D0197783

Continental Philosophy: A Very Short Introduction

'Simon Critchley succeeds in putting the 20th Century dispute between Analytical and Continental Philosophers in a nutshell. His balanced position – midway between the two Schools – is especially attractive to English-speaking readers, and the historical subtlety of his account allows it to carry more conviction than one might have thought possible.'
Stephen Toulmin, University of Southern California

'A lucid, perceptive, jargon-free introduction to Continental philosophy. Critchley packs a great deal of information, insight and wisdom into this short book.'
Richard J. Bernstein, New School University, New York

'A sensible and original account of what lies behind the phrase "Continental philosophy" which even the foes of this style of thinking will find useful.'
Pascal Engel, Université de Paris-IV-Sorbonne

Very Short Introductions available now:

ANCIENT PHILOSOPHY
  Julia Annas
THE ANGLO-SAXON AGE
  John Blair
ANIMAL RIGHTS
  David DeGrazia
ARCHAEOLOGY   Paul Bahn
ARISTOTLE   Jonathan Barnes
AUGUSTINE   Henry Chadwick
BARTHES   Jonathan Culler
THE BIBLE   John Riches
BUDDHA   Michael Carrithers
BUDDHISM   Damien Keown
CLASSICS   Mary Beard and
  John Henderson
CLAUSEWITZ   Michael Howard
CONTINENTAL PHILOSOPHY
  Simon Critchley
COSMOLOGY   Peter Coles
DARWIN   Jonathan Howard
DESCARTES   Tom Sorell
DRUGS   Leslie Iversen
EIGHTEENTH-CENTURY
  BRITAIN   Paul Langford
THE EUROPEAN UNION
  John Pinder
THE FRENCH REVOLUTION
  William Doyle
FREUD   Anthony Storr
GALILEO   Stillman Drake
GANDHI   Bhikhu Parekh
HEGEL   Peter Singer
HEIDEGGER   Michael Inwood
HINDUISM   Kim Knott
HISTORY   John H. Arnold
HOBBES   Richard Tuck
HUME   A. J. Ayer
INDIAN PHILOSOPHY
  Sue Hamilton
INTELLIGENCE   Ian J. Deary
ISLAM   Malise Ruthven
JUDAISM   Norman Solomon
JUNG   Anthony Stevens

KANT   Roger Scruton
KIERKEGAARD   Patrick Gardiner
THE KORAN   Michael Cook
LITERARY THEORY
  Jonathan Culler
LOGIC   Graham Priest
MACHIAVELLI   Quentin Skinner
MARX   Peter Singer
MEDIEVAL BRITAIN
  John Gillingham and
  Ralph A. Griffiths
MUSIC   Nicholas Cook
NIETZSCHE   Michael Tanner
NINETEENTH-CENTURY
  BRITAIN   Christopher Harvie and
  H. C. G. Matthew
PAUL   E. P. Sanders
PHILOSOPHY   Edward Craig
POLITICS   Kenneth Minogue
PSYCHOLOGY   Gillian Butler and
  Freda McManus
ROMAN BRITAIN
  Peter Salway
ROUSSEAU   Robert Wokler
RUSSELL   A. C. Grayling
RUSSIAN LITERATURE
  Catriona Kelly
THE RUSSIAN REVOLUTION
  S. A. Smith
SCHOPENHAUER
  Christopher Janaway
SHAKESPEARE   Germaine Greer
SOCIAL AND CULTURAL
  ANTHROPOLOGY
  John Monaghan and Peter Just
SOCIOLOGY   Steve Bruce
SOCRATES   C. C. W. Taylor
STUART BRITAIN   John Morrill
THEOLOGY   David F. Ford
THE TUDORS   John Guy
TWENTIETH-CENTURY
  BRITAIN   Kenneth O. Morgan
WITTGENSTEIN   A. C. Grayling

For more information visit our web site
www.oup.co.uk/vsi

Simon Critchley

CONTINENTAL PHILOSOPHY

A Very Short Introduction

OXFORD
UNIVERSITY PRESS

OXFORD

UNIVERSITY PRESS

Great Clarendon Street, Oxford OX2 6DP

Oxford University Press is a department of the University of Oxford.
It furthers the University's objective of excellence in research, scholarship,
and education by publishing worldwide in

Oxford New York

Athens Auckland Bangkok Bogotá Buenos Aires Calcutta
Cape Town Chennai Dar es Salaam Delhi Florence Hong Kong Istanbul
Karachi Kuala Lumpur Madrid Melbourne Mexico City Mumbai
Nairobi Paris São Paulo Shanghai Singapore Taipei Tokyo Toronto Warsaw

with associated companies in Berlin Ibadan

Oxford is a registered trade mark of Oxford University Press
in the UK and in certain other countries

Published in the United States
by Oxford University Press Inc., New York

British Library Cataloguing in Publication Data

Data available

Library of Congress Cataloguing in Publication Data

Data available

ISBN 0-19-285359-7

5 7 9 10 8 6 4

Typeset by RefineCatch Ltd, Bungay, Suffolk
Printed in Spain by Book Print S. L.

Contents

List of Illustrations

Preface

> Academic philosophy in England has for some time been largely limited
> to logic and theory of knowledge, and there is a tendency to confine
> philosophy to this sense and to regard its traditional association with
> general moral and intellectual systems as an error. This is a powerful but
> very local habit.
>
> Raymond Williams, *Keywords*

On 5 October 1999, when pressed for her current views on the prospect of a European union, Margaret Thatcher remarked, 'All the problems in my lifetime have come from Continental Europe, all the solutions have come from the English-speaking world'. Despite its evident falsehood, this statement expresses a deep truth: namely, that for many inhabitants of the English-speaking world, and indeed for some living outside it, there is a real divide between their world and the societies, languages, political systems, traditions, and geography of Continental Europe. British politics, especially but by no means exclusively on the right, is defined in terms of the distinction between 'Europhobes' and 'Europhiles', known to their opponents as 'Eurosceptics' and 'Eurofanatics' respectively. That is, there is a cultural distinction, some would say a divide – perhaps even an abyss – between the 'Continental' and whatever opposes it, what Baroness Thatcher, in tones deliberately reminiscent of Winston Churchill, calls 'the English-speaking world'. Continental philosophy is one expression of this cultural divide. The purpose of this short book is to explain why this has happened, why that fact is important, and what it might entail for the activity of philosophy now and in the future.

It is a matter of some contention whether Continental philosophy is a well-defined subject area in philosophy. And if one accepts that it is, then it is also a matter of dispute whether the term 'Continental philosophy' best describes this subject area (rather than, say, 'modern European philosophy', which is often employed as an alternative). Let's just say Continental philosophy is a contested concept. With this in mind, this book has a three-fold aim:

1   To show why Continental philosophy is an area of dispute by considering the history and meaning of this term and the way it is differentiated from, and represented by, what it allegedly opposes – namely analytic or Anglo-American philosophy.

2   To show how the notion of Continental philosophy can, indeed, be well defined and constitutes a distinct set of philosophical traditions and practices with a compelling range of problems all too often ignored or dismissed by the Anglo-American tradition.

3   To show, despite this, how we might in the future do better to talk about philosophy *as such* beyond such professional squabbles as to what or who is Continental or analytic.

I begin by taking a slightly different tack and sketching a larger problem that faces contemporary philosophy: the relation between wisdom and knowledge. There is a gap in much philosophy between theoretical questions of how one knows what one knows, and more practical or existential questions of what it might mean to lead a good or fulfilled human life. Much mainstream philosophy has given up the task of trying to integrate knowledge and wisdom into a single synoptic vision. I will try to show how much of the appeal of Continental philosophy lies in its attempt to bridge or reduce this gap between knowledge and wisdom (or theory and practice), thereby retaining something of an echo of the ancient definition of philosophy as the love of wisdom. But, as we shall see, in a world which is increasingly modelled on the procedures of the natural sciences, such a view is not without problems of its own.

The next few chapters can be divided in line with another classical philosophical distinction: the historical and the systematic. Chapter 2 sketches different historical ways of making the distinction between Continental and analytic philosophy. I trace Continental philosophy to the reception of the work of Immanuel Kant in the late 18th century, who in many ways is the final great figure common to both Continental and analytic traditions and also announces the parting of their ways. I shall examine why this is the case by contrasting different approaches to Kant. I shall also look in some detail at the debates which Kant's work inspired in the 1780s and 1790s, and then show how these debates establish the key issue for German idealism in the work of J. G. Fichte and G. W. F. Hegel. Crudely stated, that issue is: does Kant's critique of reason end up, completely against its express intention, undermining the basis for moral and religious belief? That is, doesn't the critique of reason, which has to be the critique of all belief, end up in a nightmare of total scepticism and nihilism? We shall follow out the considerable implications of that thought in 19th- and 20th-century Continental philosophy.

Chapter 3 begins by considering some problems with the distinction between Continental and analytic philosophy, before looking at some rather stereotypical, indeed amusing, representations of it in the literature. I then discuss two meanings of Continental philosophy: as a professional self-description used by philosophers, and as a cultural feature with a particular history used by many more people, Margaret Thatcher included. I argue that much of the hostility and misunderstanding of Continental philosophy by analytic philosophers consists in the fact that these two meanings are unhelpfully enmeshed, and that the professional self-description comes to overlay the cultural feature in often harmful ways. I then look at the history and cultural context for Continental philosophy in the English-speaking world, advancing the thesis that the conflict between philosophical traditions is best understood in terms of C. P. Snow's famous model of 'the two cultures', namely that cultural life in the English-speaking world is marked by a divide between science, on the one hand, and literature or humane understanding on the other. That is to say, Continental philosophy is not so much something foreign that takes place 'over there', but is rather the expression of an antagonism at the heart of something like 'Englishness'. I focus on the instructive historical example of John Stuart Mill in this regard and his key reflections on the English cultural divide between empiricist and speculative habits of thought, which plays out in the antagonism between the romanticism of Samuel Taylor Coleridge and the utilitarianism of Jeremy Bentham. In conclusion, I turn to other, more recent expressions of the conflict between the two cultures.

In Chapter 4 I try to lay out what is distinctive and compelling about Continental philosophy in a more systematic manner. After making some remarks on how one may account for the difference of practice amongst philosophers, I focus on the notions of tradition and history and show how these terms are interestingly understood in two philosophers: Edmund Husserl and Martin Heidegger. I propose a model for describing philosophical practice in the Continental tradition, organized around three key terms: *critique, praxis*, and *emancipation*. This aims to show how and why much Continental philosophy is concerned with giving a critique of the social practices of the modern world, a critique that aspires towards a goal of individual and societal emancipation.

I then return to the key concept of nihilism, the collapse or devaluation of the highest values, such as belief in God or the immortality of the soul, which receives its definitive articulation in the work of Friedrich Nietzsche, and I outline the interesting Russian context for Nietzsche's understanding of nihilism. I then try to show how the cultural and intellectual pathology which leads to Nietzsche's diagnosis of nihilism bifurcates after him into reactionary and progressive modernism, and how this leads to the particular understanding of the relation of philosophy to non-philosophy in the Continental tradition.

Chapter 6 deals with a specific case study. If there is one dispute that typifies the misunderstandings between Continental and analytic philosophy, then it is that which took place from the early 1930s onwards between Heidegger and Rudolf Carnap. Essentially this is a dispute between the scientific conception of the world advanced by Carnap and the Vienna Circle, and the existential or what is called 'hermeneutic' experience of the world in Heidegger. Much of the recent misunderstandings between analytic and Continental philosophers can be traced back to the curious stand-off between Heidegger and Carnap, so it is worth looking at what exactly went wrong.

In Chapter 7, I extend the discussion of the relation between a scientific and hermeneutic conception of the world by taking up the problem of *scientism* versus *obscurantism*. The fact that so much philosophy in the Continental tradition can be said to respond to a sense of crisis in the modern world, and to attempt to produce a critical consciousness of the present with an emancipatory intent, goes some way to explaining its most salient and dramatic difference from much analytic philosophy, namely its *anti-scientism*. Its critique of scientism resides in the belief that the model of the natural sciences cannot and, moreover, *should* not provide a model for philosophical method, and that the natural sciences do not provide human beings with their primary and most significant access to the world. One finds this belief expressed in a whole range of Continental thinkers, such as Henri Bergson, Husserl, Heidegger, and the philosophers associated with the Frankfurt School from the 1930s onwards. This worry about scientism is legitimate, but in recent decades it has also risked being conflated with an anti-scientific attitude. This is the risk of *obscurantism*. In my view, the two poles that are to be avoided in philosophy are scientism and obscurantism, which reflect pernicious tendencies within both analytic and Continental philosophy, as the debate between Carnap and Heidegger eloquently shows. As an alternative to the two extremes of scientism and obscurantism, present in both analytic and Continental philosophy, I propose a 'third way' between these two extremes.

I conclude the book with some ruminations about what I continue to see as the promise of philosophy. The current divisions in the study of philosophy are a consequence of certain inadequate and sectarian professional self-descriptions (are you an analytic, post-analytic, Continental, or modern European philosopher?). Both Continental and analytic philosophy are, to a great extent, sectarian self-descriptions that are the consequence of the professionalization of the discipline, a professionalization that, in my view, has led to the weakening of philosophy's critical function and to its progressive marginalization in the life of culture. My view is that philosophy should be a vital expression of that life.

A couple of provisos and a word of thanks before we begin. My aim has been to keep references to a minimum to focus on conveying the key ideas as simply as possible. This means that in many places I crib or borrow other philosophers' arguments and ideas, and indeed sometimes ideas of my own that I have published elsewhere. I make no apologies for this, as this book is intended for the intellectually curious but decidedly non-specialist reader. The References and Further Reading sections at the end of the book are intended to reveal my sources and to provide interested readers with an idea of where they might go next.

You will not find in this book a survey or summary of all the thinkers, traditions, and movements that make up what we think of as Continental philosophy. As such, there are significant gaps in my coverage. Such summaries already exist, some of them are very good, and it has not been my intention to add to their number. Rather, this book is more of an argued reflection about the nature of philosophy in the Continental tradition, and the style is that of the essay, not the textbook. In other words, what follows is an idiosyncratic view of matters.

This book was initially drafted between March and May 2000, when I had the good fortune to hold the Visiting Lectureship in Philosophy at the University of Sydney, and the finished text is based on my lecture notes. I mention this because of the following coincidence: on the day I arrived in Sydney, 1 March 2000, the Departments of 'General' and 'Traditional and Modern' Philosophy at the University of Sydney were reunited as a single Department of Philosophy after 27 years of divorce. Now, although this divorce – which was not without acrimony it appears, an acrimony which, it must be said, has not disappeared without trace – had its origins in political differences, essentially the participation of Australia in the Vietnam War in the early 1970s, it also had its intellectual differences, most significantly the relation of philosophy to politics, in particular Marxism and feminism. Although it is not accurate to say that the division between departments was explicable in terms of the analytic–Continental split, the latter certainly came to overlay this division in all sorts of more or less egregious ways. I would like to thank my friends, colleagues, and, most of all, my students in Sydney for helping me rethink this division. Finally, this book was not my idea, but that of my wonderful editor at Oxford University Press, Shelley Cox. I would like to thank her for having such good ideas.

Chapter 1

The Gap between Knowledge and Wisdom

Philosophy is the love of wisdom. If you think that you are in love with wisdom, then philosophy is presumably the subject to study. But what is the wisdom that philosophy teaches? For Socrates, and for nearly all ancient philosophers that came after him, the wisdom that philosophy teaches concerns what it might mean to lead a good human life. It was axiomatic for much ancient philosophy that a good human life would also be a happy one. In this picture, which finds its definitive expression in Aristotle, but which is assumed by later Hellenistic schools like the Stoics, philosophy would allow the attainment of the highest happiness, namely the life of disinterested contemplation. So, philosophy is the reflective life, the examined life, the assumption being that the unexamined life is not worth living. Philosophy should form human beings and not just inform them.

But it should not be forgotten that although the unexamined life is not worth living, the unlived life is not worth examining, and philosophy for the ancients was not divorced from the practical to and fro of everyday social life. Rather, philosophy as a reflective practice of examining what passes for truth in the name of truth is something that took place in what the ancient Greeks called the *polis*, the public realm of political life. Philosophy was an eminently *practical* activity, which is markedly different from the overwhelmingly theoretical enquiry it has become since the 17th century.

1. Giacinto Brandi (1621–91), 'Allegory of Philosophy'

In the ancient picture, the wisdom that philosophy teaches us to love is identical with the pursuit of the good life, a life of reflection and contemplation that would, by definition, be a happy life. Now, strangely perhaps, it is this model that most people *outside* philosophy – that is, outside the academic study of philosophy – think that most people *inside* philosophy are in the grip of. This is why they quite naturally assume that philosophy's central question must be the meaning of life. With this thought in mind, imagine the following scene: the professional philosopher meets a stranger at a party and in response to the question 'so what do *you* do?', she replies, and the stranger, momentarily emboldened and otherwise at a loss for anything to say, asks, 'so what's the meaning of life then?'. At this point, a little nervous giggling is followed by the philosopher's anxious attempt to either change the subject as quickly as possible or to explain with an embarrassed smile that the academic study of philosophy is not really about such things. Now, as awkward as I find this situation socially, I think that the stranger is quite justified in their assumption. That is, if philosophy does not deal with – not necessarily answer, but at least tackle – the question of the meaning of life, then philosophers cannot be said to be doing their job properly.

In my view, the problem here is not so much with people outside philosophy as with people inside philosophy, our professional philosophers. For most of us, the very idea that philosophy might be concerned with the question of the meaning of life or the attainment of a good and happy human life is something of a joke, and furthermore a joke in rather poor taste. Such questions are relegated to the realm of what is patronizingly called 'folk psychology'. For the most part, professional philosophy has happily conceded this terrain to the vast and ever-rising tide of books on 'mind, body, and spirit', those rows of brightly coloured New Age titles that sit embarrassingly near the ever-shrinking philosophy sections in high street book stores. Professional philosophy has largely given up such battles and taken early retirement.

With what, then, *is* philosophy concerned for most professional philosophers, if it is not concerned with wisdom? Let's say it is concerned with *knowledge*. Knowledge of what? At its broadest, we might say that philosophy is concerned with knowledge of how things are the way they are. The Latin word for knowledge – *scientia* – is illuminating here. The question of knowledge, of knowing how things are the way they are, is a scientific one. It is science, modern natural science, that provides us with the best and most reliable knowledge of how things are the way they are. Why? Because natural science can offer empirical proof for its hypotheses, it can verify its claims. If I say, 'Jesus Christ is the redeemer of humankind', and offer no empirical proof, then whether I accept the claim or not is wholly a matter a faith. But if I say that the substance of water is characterized by having at all times two parts hydrogen to one part oxygen, then I can show this in an experiment to prove the result.

As we are all acutely aware, we live in a scientific world, a world where we are expected to provide empirical evidence for our claims or find those claims rightly rejected. The scientific conception of the world, which dates back to the early decades of the 17th century in England and France, dominates the way we see things and, perhaps even more importantly, the way we *expect* to see things. We expect to see things somewhat like spectators in a theatre where we can inspect them theoretically – the Greek word for a theatre spectator is a *theoros*. Things are present as objects that are empirically and immediately given in the form of sensations or representations. Science gives us knowledge of the nature of such things. These things are then called 'facts'.

In a science-dominated world, what role does our professional philosopher assign to philosophy? This can in part be answered by recalling the Greek word for knowledge, *episteme*. Philosophy becomes *epistemology*, the theory of knowledge. That is, it is overwhelmingly concerned with logical and methodological questions as to *how* we know what we know, and in virtue of what such knowledge is valid. Philosophy becomes a theoretical enquiry into the conditions under which scientific knowledge is possible. In the scientific conception of the world, the role of philosophy moves from being, as it was for Plato, the queen of the sciences, where theoretical knowledge was unified with practical wisdom. It becomes rather, in John Locke's formula at the beginning of *An Essay Concerning Human Understanding* in 1689, an under-labourer to science, whose job is to clear away the rubbish that lies in the way to knowledge and scientific progress. Philosophers become janitors in the Crystal Palace of the sciences.

The job of a janitor is respectable enough, but what of the question of wisdom? The problem here is that science is wonderful: it provides us with a truer, better account of the way things are, what contemporary philosophers are fond of calling a 'naturalistic ontology'. Furthermore, through the work of science's helpmeet, technology, our lives have been transformed and improved to an extent unimaginable to someone from the ancient world, or even indeed to our great-grandparents. Science is therefore not only wonderful, it is effective. Yet, despite this – or perhaps because of it – the question of wisdom still nags at us, it still irritates like an appendix we believed we no longer needed.

The question is: does the scientific conception of the world eradicate the need for an answer to the question of the meaning of life? Does the body of knowledge require the appendectomy of wisdom? In a certain extreme view it does, and some philosophers might argue that all questions must either be answerable through empirical enquiry or be rejected as spurious. As such, it might be claimed, the question of the meaning of life can be answered causally or empirically through Darwinian evolutionary theory. In this picture, life is explicable on the basis of certain causal hypotheses, such as natural selection: that is, human cognition is the outcome of evolutionary dispositions. There is even a branch of philosophy called 'evolutionary epistemology' that attempts first to reduce all philosophical questions to epistemological questions, and secondly to claim that all such questions have to be answered with reference to evolutionary dispositions.

I take a less extreme view of the relation between knowledge and wisdom, or between scientific enquiry and what we might call humanistic enquiry. I do not think that the question of the meaning of life is reducible to empirical investigation. It is just not a causal matter. There is, I think, a gap between knowledge and wisdom: not an explanatory gap that might be closed by producing a better, more comprehensive theory, but more of a *felt* gap. If all epistemic worries are to be resolved empirically by scientific enquiry, then we might feel that even if – one fine and beautiful morning – all those worries were resolved, then this would somehow still be irrelevant to the question of wisdom, to the question of knowing in what exactly a good human life might consist.

The paradox – and it is a massive paradox of everyday experience, that we will meet in Chapter 2 as the paradox of nihilism – is that the scientific conception of the world does not close the gap between knowledge and wisdom, but makes us feel it all the more acutely. I would even wager that this paradox is at its most acute in scientifically and technologically highly developed societies. It is in advanced Western societies that the gap between knowledge and wisdom seems to widen into an abyss. In this sense, the speculative question of the meaning of life is a consequence of luxury and affluence. Perhaps it was ever thus – philosophy only arises once the basic exigencies of life have been provided. As Bertolt Brecht said, 'food first, then ethics'. True enough. But the curious fact about human beings is that when you give them food, even more food than they can eat, when you shower them with every earthly blessing, then they will concoct new miseries for themselves, new neuroses and pathologies, and even a new 'science' to deal with those new neuroses and pathologies: psychoanalysis, psychotherapy, aromatherapy, reflexology, or whatever. It is when the force of this paradox begins to be felt existentially that the neglected question of the meaning of life comes back with a real and frightening vengeance: 'I seem to have everything I need and want, but what is the point of my life?'

This curious but utterly everyday state of affairs is the justified source of many of the, in my view, unjustified attempts to fill the 'meaning gap' and answer the question of the meaning of life. This can be done in many ways: through a return to traditional religion, or through the invention of a new religion; through political authoritarianism, which is often combined with a return to traditional religion in a heady cocktail (for example, Serbian nationalism); or through the 57 varieties of filling the meaning gap that are currently available in the supermarket of esotericism: astrology, yoga, sitting under pyramids holding crystals, finding your inner child, or whatever. As we will see towards the end of this little book, these are varieties of *obscurantism*. That is, if what is mistaken in much contemporary philosophy is its infatuation with science, which leads to scientism, then the equally mistaken rejection of science leads to obscurantism. One of my closing claims will be that there is a risk of obscurantism in some contemporary Continental philosophy. So, if the risk of contemporary philosophy is scientism, then its obverse reflection is obscurantism. In John Stuart Mill's words, 'the one doctrine is accused of making men beasts, the other lunatics'.

So, to recapitulate a little, ancient philosophy was characterized, amongst other things, by an identity, or at least an attempted integration, of knowledge and wisdom: namely, that a knowledge of how things were the way they were would lead to wisdom in the conduct of one's life. The assumption that ties knowledge and wisdom together is the idea that the cosmos as such expresses a human purpose, and therefore that knowledge of nature would be part and parcel of what it means to be human. This is what is called the 'teleological view of the universe', where each natural thing can be explained in terms of what Aristotle called its final cause, that goal for the sake of which a thing is the way it is. Such a view allowed for a felicitous unity of theory and practice, of knowledge and wisdom, of causal explanation and existential understanding or meaning, where, for example, nature can be seen as a living book written by the hand of God.

In the modern world, through the extraordinary progress of the sciences from the 17th century to the present, this unity has split apart. René Descartes is already writing in 1641, in *Meditations on First Philosophy*, 'the customary search for final causes is utterly useless in physics'. The universe expresses no human purpose, it is simply governed by physical laws that we can do our best to ascertain, but which are indifferent to human striving. The universe is vast, cold, inhuman, and mechanical. This is why Blaise Pascal, writing at the time of the emergence of this transformed world-view in the late 1650s, says that 'the eternal silence of infinite spaces fills me with dread'. That is, *knowledge* of the infinite, open universe of Copernicus and Galileo, without meaning or final purpose, inspires sheer anxiety when one turns to the question of *wisdom*. This is one expression of the historical and spiritual experience that is known as the *Enlightenment*: we are left with an experiential gap between the realms of knowledge and wisdom, truth and meaning, theory and practice, causal explanation and existential understanding. As Max Weber expresses it some two and a half centuries later, the scientific revolution, in its undeniable truth, produced a *disenchantment of nature*. Nature is no longer the visible expression of some 'world soul' in which humans also participate. Rather, nature is sheer, impersonal objective 'stuff', which is law governed, causally explicable, but completely cut adrift from human intentions.

If that is so, then the problem for us moderns is clear: in the face of the disenchantment of nature brought about by the scientific revolution, we experience a gap between knowledge and wisdom that has the consequence of divesting our lives of meaning. The question is: can nature or indeed human selves become *re-enchanted* in such a way that reduces or even eliminates the meaning gap and produces some plausible conception of a good life? The dilemma seems to be intractable: on the one hand, the philosophical cost of scientific truth seems to be scientism, in which case we become beasts. On the other hand, the rejection of scientism through a new humanization of the cosmos seems to lead to obscurantism, in which case we become lunatics. Neither side of this alternative is particularly attractive. Towards the end of this book, I will try and suggest a middle path.

But what, you may well ask, has this got to do with Continental philosophy? My contention is that what philosophy should be thinking through at present is this dilemma which on the one side threatens to turn us into beasts, and on the other side into lunatics. This means that the question of wisdom, and its related question of the meaning of life, should at the very least move closer to the centre of philosophical activity and not be treated with indifference, embarrassment, or even contempt. The appeal of much that goes under the name of Continental philosophy, in my view, is that it attempts to unify or at least move closer together questions of knowledge and wisdom, of philosophical truth and existential meaning. Examples are legion here, whether one thinks of Hegel on the life and death struggle for recognition as part and parcel of the ascent to absolute knowing; Nietzsche on the death of God and the need for a revaluation of values; Karl Marx on the alienation of human beings under conditions of capitalism and the requirement for an emancipatory and equitable social transformation; Freud on the unconscious repression at work in dreams, jokes, and slips of the tongue and what that reveals about the irrationality at the heart of mental life; Heidegger on anxiety, the deadening indifference of inauthentic social life, and the need for an authentic existence; Sartre on bad faith, nausea, and the useless but necessary passion of human freedom; Albert Camus on the question of suicide in a universe rendered absurd by the death of God; Emmanuel Levinas on the trauma of our infinite responsibilities to others. This list could be extended.

2. Frederico Zuccari (1540–1609), 'Wisdom'

That is, the appeal of Continental philosophy is that it seems closer to the grain and detail of human existence. It seems truer to the drama of life, to the stuff of human hopes and fears, and the many little woes and weals to which our flesh is prone. Of course, that is not to say that such concerns are entirely absent from mainstream Anglo-American or analytic philosophy. Although it might be fair to say, in my terms, that much of the latter is dominated by the question of knowledge, conceived scientifically or naturalistically, at the expense of the question of wisdom, this would not explain a figure like Ludwig Wittgenstein, for example, whose enormous appeal as a thinker might be said to be based on the way philosophical truth comes together with a certain conception of existential meaning, indeed a certain way of life. That is, the animating desire of Wittgenstein's work might be said to be therapeutic. So, let's say that the attempt to bridge the gap between knowledge and wisdom is not a sufficient condition for discriminating between analytic and Continental philosophy. That is not the issue. My general point is that the attempt to bridge that gap should be a necessary condition for *all* philosophizing.

Chapter 2
Origins of Continental Philosophy: How to get from Kant to German Idealism

The task of the next few chapters is to define Continental philosophy and then to bring out what is distinctive and compelling about it. I would like to do this in a two-fold manner: historically and systematically. Chapters 2 and 3 will consider historical development, whereas in Chapter 4 I offer a more argued, systematic account of Continental philosophy. The idea of writing the history of philosophy with a systematic, argumentative intent has been a very common way of proceeding in the Continental tradition since Hegel's 1807 masterpiece, *Phenomenology of Spirit*, which unifies both approaches. One can also find the same approach employed in more contemporary work, such as Jürgen Habermas's *Knowledge and Human Interests* (1968), Foucault's *Madness and Civilization* (1961), and Derrida's *Of Grammatology* (1967). It is much less common in the Anglo-American tradition.

Husserl or Kant? Two ways of beginning Continental philosophy

Let me begin by considering two different ways of distinguishing Continental from analytic philosophy. One could imagine a book on Continental philosophy that would begin the history of the subject around 1900 with the publication of Husserl's *Logical Investigations*, what Heidegger calls the 'breakthrough' work that begins the tradition

What is Continental Philosophy?

Continental philosophy is the name for a 200-year period in the history of philosophy that begins with the publication of Kant's critical philosophy in the 1780s. This led on to the following key movements:

1 German idealism and romanticism and its aftermath (Fichte, Schelling, Hegel, Schlegel and Novalis, Schleiermacher, Schopenhauer)

2 The critique of metaphysics and the 'masters of suspicion' (Feuerbach, Marx, Nietzsche, Freud, Bergson)

3 Germanophone phenomenology and existential philosophy (Husserl, Max Scheler, Karl Jaspers, Heidegger)

4 French phenomenology, Hegelianism, and anti-Hegelianism (Kojève, Sartre, Merleau-Ponty, Levinas, Bataille, de Beauvoir)

5 Hermeneutics (Dilthey, Gadamer, Ricoeur)

6 Western Marxism and the Frankfurt School (Lukacs, Benjamin, Horkheimer, Adorno, Marcuse, Habermas)

7 French structuralism (Lévi-Strauss, Lacan, Althusser), post-structuralism (Foucault, Derrida, Deleuze), post-modernism (Lyotard, Baudrillard), and feminism (Irigaray, Kristeva)

of what is called phenomenology. Such an approach would have the virtue of reminding readers that the contemporary division (or indeed gulf) between analytic and Continental philosophy is essentially a division between the traditions inspired by Gottlob Frege's revolutionary philosophy of logic and language – such as the early Wittgenstein, Viennese logical positivism, and Anglo-American philosophy of language – and those traditions derived from an often critical confrontation with Husserl's phenomenology – such as existentialism and deconstruction. There was significant contact between Frege and Husserl, and in 1894 Frege published a penetrating review of Husserl's first book, *Philosophy of Arithmetic* (1891), that had the effect of dramatically altering Husserl's views on the relation of logic to psychology: namely, that logic cannot, as the early Husserl thought, be reduced to psychology.

Of course, what is peculiar about these seemingly divergent traditions of analytic philosophy and phenomenology is that they have a common Central European ancestry in the work of the Prague-based philosopher Bernard Bolzano and Franz Brentano, who was professor in Vienna and counted the young Sigmund Freud amongst his students. In brief, what Frege and Husserl took from Bolzano is the idea that thoughts are not subjective mental experiences, but have an objective content that is capable of analysis. Whereas what is taken from Franz Brentano is the intentionality thesis: namely that every thought is directed towards objects in the world and not locked up in some cabinet of consciousness. These two ideas fuelled the rejection of scepticism, relativism, and what was called 'psychologism', the view developed in Germany in the early 19th century that all logical and philosophical problems are reducible to psychological mechanisms. Husserl held to a psychologistic account of logic and arithmetic until Frege persuaded him otherwise. It is the critique of psychologism, as well as the categorical rejection of any attempt to reduce philosophy to empirical science, that unites Frege's philosophy of language and Husserl's phenomenology. So, by this account, the origins of analytic philosophy have the same historical vintage as the origins of Continental philosophy, have a similar geographical source in German-speaking Central Europe, and share a common philosophical enemy. The only way to re-establish communication amongst philosophers is by going back to the historical and conceptual point where the traditions diverged.

This is Michael Dummett's strategy in his influential 1993 book *Origins of Analytical Philosophy*. Dummett recounts the history of analytic philosophy from Frege onwards in the laudable hope that a clearer understanding of the philosophical past will be a precondition for some sort of mutual comprehension between contemporary philosophers. The contemporary situation is described by Dummett in suitably grim terms:

> I do not mean to pretend that philosophy in the two traditions is basically the same; obviously that would be ridiculous. We can re-establish communication only by going back to the point of divergence. It's no use now shouting across the gulf. It is obvious that philosophers will never reach agreement. It is a pity, however, if they can no longer talk to one another or understand one another. It is difficult to achieve such understanding, because if you think people are on the wrong track, you may have no great desire to talk with them or to take the trouble to criticize their views. But we have reached a point at which it is as if we're working in different subjects.

As such, the contemporary philosophical context contrasts extremely unfavourably with that at the beginning of the 20th century. Dummett writes,

> Frege was the grandfather of analytical philosophy, Husserl the founder of the phenomenological school, two radically different philosophical movements. In 1903, say, how would they have appeared to any German student of philosophy who knew the work of both? Not, certainly, as two deeply opposed thinkers: rather as remarkably close in orientation, despite some divergence of interests.

Dummett then goes on, intriguingly, to compare Frege and Husserl to the Rhine and the Danube, 'which arise quite close to each other and for a time pursue roughly parallel paths, only to diverge in utterly different directions and flow into different seas'. Although it is clear, for

Dummett at least, that Frege's Rhine is the right course for thought (while Husserl's Danube debouches into the idealist Black Sea of the Continental tradition), this is an instructive and suggestive image which rather nicely destabilizes the distinction between philosophical traditions.

Dummett's strategy is compelling, and I will implicitly use it in my discussion of the conflict between the scientific and hermeneutic conceptions of the world in Chapter 6: namely that one way of achieving mutual comprehension between partisans in this conflict is by tracing it back to its philosophical source in the stand-off between Heidegger and Carnap. However – and this is the second way of making the distinction between traditions – if we are to understand the nature of philosophy in the Continental tradition, then I believe it is necessary to begin with Kant, who, as I said above, is the final great figure common to both analytic and Continental philosophy and who announces the parting of their ways. To begin with, there are two rather simple reasons for beginning with Kant rather than Husserl: first, 20th-century developments in Continental philosophy are largely unintelligible without reference to their 19th-century precursors, especially Hegel, Marx, and Nietzsche. This is particularly the case with French philosophy since the 1930s, which might well be described in terms of a series of returns to Hegel (in the work of Alexandre Kojève and the early Jean-Paul Sartre), Nietzsche (in Michel Foucault and Gilles Deleuze), or Marx (in Louis Althusser). Second, the history of 19th-century non-Anglophone philosophy is, in Britain at least, woefully under-represented in undergraduate syllabuses, where it is still possible to receive a degree in philosophy without having read much, if anything, of Germanophone philosophy between Kant and Frege. It is therefore still necessary to try and fill this gap.

Two ways of reading Kant

Much of the difference between analytic and Continental philosophy simply turns on *how* one reads Kant and *how much* Kant one reads. That is, whether one is solely preoccupied with the epistemological issues of the First Critique or *Critique of Pure Reason* (1781), or by the greater systematic ambitions of the Third Critique or *Critique of the Power of Judgement* (1790). I would like to explore this thought in a little more depth.

If one focuses on the First Critique, then one is usually concerned with the success of the argument of the transcendental deduction: here Kant tries to show that in order to experience objects at all we have to presuppose the operations of what he calls the 'categories of the understanding' and hence a human subject who understands, that is, who unifies the blooming, buzzing confusion of perceptual experience under concepts. Thus, as Kant puts it, 'objects conform to concepts and not concepts to objects'. Such a reading of Kant will be guided by the question of whether he successfully provides a valid foundation or grounding for empirical knowledge and meets the challenge of the scepticism of David Hume. Kant claimed that Hume awoke him from his 'dogmatic slumber' by showing that if we take the sceptical challenge seriously, then we can never be sure whether our concepts, based as they are in fleeting sensations and impressions, adequately correspond to objects in themselves and produce knowledge. Kant's response is to turn the whole issue round by acknowledging that, although we can never know things-in-themselves, the objects of our representations conform to the concepts we have of them in a manner sufficient for knowledge. This turning round is what Kant calls the 'Copernican turn' in philosophy. The empirical world is indeed real for us, but in order to explain how we make sense of the world we have to presuppose logically, or in Kant's parlance 'transcendentally', a subject or consciousness that unites intuitions under concepts. This is the rough shape of the thesis that is called 'transcendental idealism', a thesis that

Immanuel Kant.

Geb. d. 22. Apr. 1724 zu Königsberg in Preußen, gest. d. 12. Febr. 1804 ebenda.

Der Königsberger Weltweise; Begründer einer neuen philosophischen Aera; voll tiefer Natur=Menschen= und Geschichtskenntniß. Er zieht in seiner „Kritik der reinen Vernunft" dieser ihre Grenze und beweist, daß metaphysisches Wissen, also jede Speculation über Willensfreiheit Unsterblichkeit und Gott, unmöglich sei, gelangt aber zu diesen höchsten Ideen auf dem Gebiete der Sittlichkeit durch den praktischen Gebrauch der reinen Vernunft in Auffindung der ihr erfahrungsgemäs zugänglichen Sittengesetze, und der Folgerungen daraus. In seinen Hauptwerken trocken und schwerverständlich, ist er in seinen sonstigen Schriften, wie es auch sein freier begeisteter Vortrag war, lebendig, voll Witz und Laune.

3. Engraving of Immanuel Kant (1724–1804)

Kant thinks is consistent with empirical realism. Read in this light, Kant's major philosophical contribution is to epistemology and, by implication, philosophy of science. Indeed, this was how he was overwhelmingly read by the school of Neo-Kantianism that dominated German and French academic philosophy between 1890 and the late 1920s. It was this epistemological reading of Kant in the work of Peter Strawson and others that dominated the Anglo-American reception of Kant until fairly recently.

However, the ambition of the Third Critique is rather different. Kant attempts to construct a bridge between the faculties of the understanding (the domain of epistemology whose concern is knowledge of nature) and reason (the domain of ethics whose concern is freedom), through a critique of the faculty of judgement. Judgement would be the mediator between the realms of nature and freedom and would harmonize the elements of the critical philosophy into a system. If one takes this route, then the burning issue of Kant's philosophy becomes the plausibility of the relation of pure and practical reason, nature and freedom, or the unity of theory and practice. As we will see below, this is precisely the route followed by German idealism in Fichte, F. W. J. Schelling, Hegel, and in early German romanticism in Friedrich Schlegel and Novalis. Arguably, it is this route that Continental philosophy has followed ever since.

Kant and Hamann – the critique of pure reason and the need for a meta-critique of that purity

Let me try to explain how we get from Kant to German idealism in a little more detail by trying to reconstruct some of the context for post-Kantian philosophy. The entire project of the German Enlightenment, the *Aufklärung*, which was based on the sovereignty of reason, suffered a sort of internal collapse. The problem can be simply described: the sovereignty of reason consists in the claim that reason can criticize all our beliefs. As Kant writes in the preface to the first edition of the First Critique,

> Our age is, to a preeminent degree, the age of criticism, and to criticism all our beliefs must submit. Religion in its holiness, and the state in its majesty, cannot exempt themselves from its tribunal without arousing just suspicion against themselves.

But if that is true – if reason can criticize all things – then surely it must also criticize itself. Therefore, there has to be a *meta-critique* of critique if the critique is to be truly effective. This is the view of Kant's most influential early critic and fellow resident of Königsberg, Johann Georg Hamann, who coined the concept *Metakritik*, still a very common term in German philosophy. If Kant represents and tries to defend the rationalism of the Enlightenment, then Hamann's is the voice of the counter-Enlightenment that would flower in the aesthetic and cultural movements of *Sturm und Drang* (storm and stress) and early German romanticism. Hamann underwent a dramatic religious conversion after some interesting homosexual adventures during a failed business trip to London in 1758. The account of Hamann's subsequent relationship with Kant, where the latter was engaged by Hamann's former employer in Riga to bring the reborn religious enthusiast back to the path of reason, is the stuff of the very best historical novels.

But I digress. In 1784 Hamann wrote his *Metacritique of the Purism of Reason*, where he criticized Kant for formalism, namely for his overvaluation of the formal character of knowledge, and for the belief that reason could be separated from experience, the a priori could be divorced from the a posteriori. Hamann's critique foreshadows that of his friend, and indeed longtime housemate, Freidrich Heinrich Jacobi, as well as that of Hegel, and takes the following shape: that Kant's critical philosophy breaks down into a series of vicious dualisms (form versus content, sensibility versus understanding, reason versus experience, nature versus freedom, the pure versus the practical, and so on), and

4. Portrait of Johann Georg Hamann (1730–88)

that the primacy of practical reason is a mere empty formalism of abstract duty. For Hamann, in another uncanny prediction of later philosophical developments, namely the linguistic turn, the separation between reason and experience, or form and content, is impossible because thought depends on language, which is, of course, a mixture of both. Where exactly do you draw the distinction between concepts and intuitions in the actual use of language? He writes 'not only does the entire capacity to think rest upon language . . . but language is also in the middle of the misunderstanding of reason with itself'.

So, if reason must criticize all things, there must also be a meta-critique of reason. But if that is so, then what prevents this meta-critique from becoming scepticism, radical and total scepticism? As Frederick Beiser remarks, 'A nightmare looms: that the self-criticism of reason ends in nihilism, doubt about the existence of everything. That fear was the sum and substance of the crisis of the *Aufklärung*'. As I will try and argue below, it is the concept of nihilism that best permits one to distinguish analytic and Continental philosophy. This issue was at the core of two hugely important conflicts in the late 18th century in Germany, and Jacobi was at the centre of both: the pantheism conflict and the atheism conflict.

The pantheism and atheism conflicts – Jacobi's implications

The pantheism conflict began with the publication of Jacobi's *Letters on Spinoza's Doctrine* in 1785, which was his correspondence with Moses Mendelssohn concerning G. E. Lessing's shocking late confession of Spinozism. Most of the best minds of the time participated in this conflict, including Mendelssohn, Kant, Johann Herder, Johann Wolfgang von Goethe, and Hamann. Baruch de Spinoza was ridiculously caricatured until the time of this conflict as either some sort of rationalistic pantheist or, worse, a satanic atheist. This conflict had the side effect of putting an end to that caricature, culminating in Novalis's description of Spinoza as the '*Gott vertrunkene Mensch*' ('the God-drunken man'), but that was not the real issue at stake. Jacobi uses Lessing's admission of Spinozism to provide a visceral critique of the *Aufklärung*, or Enlightenment. Jacobi's point is, first, that Spinoza's philosophy is the paradigm of rationalism, and furthermore that the latter, if consistently adhered to, leads to atheism. So, contra Kant the *Aufklärer*, reason leads to the collapse of any basis for religious belief or moral life. If that is so, Jacobi adds, then we have a clear, and rather stark, choice to make: either to embrace the rational atheism of Enlightenment, or to reject it through an irrational leap of faith. Jacobi finds an inspiration for this in his reading of Pascal for whom 'nothing is so consistent with reason as this denial of reason'. Namely, that the correct exercise of reason is brought to the point where we have to recognize what lies beyond it: the domain of faith. Jacobi's version of Pascal's wager was also decisive for another later religious critic of secular rationalism, Søren Kierkegaard. The question of the status of reason and rationality versus the irrationality of much of human existence is a conflict that is at the heart of disagreements in the Continental tradition to this day, for example in the modernism/postmodernism debate that defined much of the 1980s and early 1990s. Beiser rightly concludes, 'It is no exaggeration to say that this controversy set one of the defining issues of the whole Continental tradition, the problem of the authority of reason. The so-called "post-modern predicament" really began, then, in 1786'.

The other issue that determines the path of Continental philosophy is the atheist conflict, which began in 1798, and which led in 1799 to the removal of Fichte from the chair of philosophy at the University of Jena on the charge of atheism. The origins of this conflict lie in the publication of various anonymous scurrilous pamphlets in 1798, which followed the publication of journal articles by Fichte and the now little known Friedrich C. Forberg on the status of religion and morals. The story of Fichte's dismissal is a rather seedy and sorry affair, which bears some comparison with Bertrand Russell's own atheist conflict in New

5. Portrait of Freidrich Heinrich Jacobi (1743–1819)

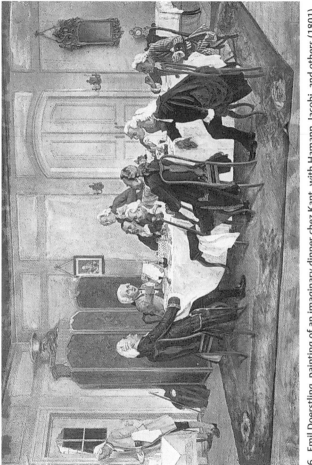

6. Emil Doerstling, painting of an imaginary dinner chez Kant, with Hamann, Jacobi, and others (1801)

York in 1940, where he was prevented from taking up his position at City College, New York on the basis of a campaign of character assassination waged against him for his professed atheism and liberal views on sexual morals. Lord Russell was described by Joseph Goldstein, attorney for Mrs Jean Kay, who led the campaign against Russell, as 'lecherous, libidinous, lustful, venerous, erotomaniac, aphrodisiac, irreverent, narrow minded, untruthful, and bereft of moral fibre'. Praise indeed! But philosophers from the time of Socrates have been condemned with corrupting the morals of the youth. Now, although Jena in the 1790s was not exactly Manhattan in the 1940s, it should be remembered that it was the philosophical centre of intellectual life in Germany during this period, home of many of the greatest minds of the time (Fichte, the Schlegel brothers, Novalis, Schelling), and the crucible out of which Early German or Jena Romanticism was born.

Although the historical detail of the debate is both interesting and slightly depressing, it becomes philosophically substantial when Jacobi weighs in in 1799 with his *Letter to Fichte*. In this text, we find the first philosophical employment of the concept of *nihilism*. For Jacobi, simply stated, Fichte's position, known as Fichtean idealism, is nihilism. What he means by this must be understood with reference to the deflationary effects of the Kantian critique of traditional metaphysics outlined above, which not only denied human beings cognitive access to the speculative objects of classical metaphysics (God, the soul), but also removes the possibility of knowing both things-in-themselves and what Kant described as the 'noumenal' ground of the self, having no phenomenal presence. Jacobi's basic thesis is that Fichte's reworking of Kantian transcendental idealism leads to an impoverished *egoism* which has no knowledge of objects or subjects in themselves. It is nihilistic because it allows the existence of nothing outside or apart from the ego, and the ego is itself nothing but a product of the 'free power of imagination'. Jacobi protests, in an extraordinary passage,

If the highest upon which I can reflect, what I can contemplate, is my empty and pure, naked and mere ego, with its autonomy and freedom: then rational self-contemplation, then rationality is for me a curse – I deplore my existence.

Against what he sees as the monism of Fichtean idealism, Jacobi argues for a form of philosophical dualism, where beyond the philosophical preoccupation with truth *(die Wahrheit)* lies the sphere of the true *(das Wahre)*, which is only accessible to faith or the heart. Once again, Jacobi's critique of Fichte is strongly reminiscent of Pascal's critique of Descartes, where nihilism is the accusation levelled by a Christian world-view at a secularizing rationalism. Thus, the existential choice that faces us, which cannot be rationally proven but upon which we must wager, is between Fichtean idealism, which is nihilistic because it offers knowledge of nothing outside of the ego's projections, and Jacobian dualism, which he describes self-mockingly as 'chimerism' because it claims that God is the essence of reason without being able to demonstrate this rationally. Jacobi concludes,

But the human being has such a choice, this single one: Nothingness or a God. Choosing Nothingness, he makes himself into a God; that is, he makes an apparition into God because if there is no God, it is impossible that man and everything which surrounds him is not merely an apparition. I repeat: God is, and is outside of me, a living being, existing in itself, or I am God. There is no third.

In denying God we risk turning the human being into God. That is, there is a Promethean temptation in Kantian and Fichtean idealism, where the human being turns into some replica of God, creating from nothing (it is worth recalling that Mary Shelley's novel, *Frankenstein* (1819), was subtitled *The Modern Prometheus*, where something monstrous stalks the scientific rationalism of the Enlightenment).

To show some of the implications of this thought in the Continental tradition, let me give a couple of further examples. If nihilism is the accusation of philosophical egoism, where all that was solid in the pre-Kantian world-view melts into air, then one finds a bizarre confirmation of Jacobi's critique in the egoism of Max Stirner's extraordinary book, *The Ego and its Own* (1844), the book that was subjected to a long and withering critique by Marx and Friedrich Engels in *The German Ideology* (1846). What is denigrated by Jacobi as nihilism is anarchistically celebrated by Stirner as individual liberation. If I am nothing, Stirner argues, then 'I am not nothing in the sense of emptiness, but I am the creative nothing, the nothing out of which I myself as creator create everything'. As the perverse consequence of his attempt to show that Hegel's and Ludwig Feuerbach's critiques of religion are still fatally entangled with religious modes of thinking, Stirner answers the question 'what is man?' by transforming the ego into a replica of God. The human being becomes the self-caused cause, the *causa sui* of medieval theology. To anticipate the existentialism of Sartre, in whom Stirner finds a curious echo a century later, in a godless, nihilistic world human beings are possessed of a passionate freedom to become godlike. This is why Sartre concludes *Being and Nothingness* by stating that 'man is a useless passion'.

One also finds an echo of Jacobi's version of Pascal's wager in Fyodor Dostoevsky's depiction of Kirilov the nihilist in his novel *The Devils* (1871).

> Everyone who desires supreme freedom must dare to kill himself. He who dares to kill himself has learnt the secret of the deception. Beyond that there is no freedom; that's all, and beyond it there is nothing. He who dares to kill himself is a god. Now every one can make it so that there shall be no God and there shall be nothing. But no one has done so yet.

Such is the position that Dostoevsky describes as 'logical suicide'. That is, as he puts it in his diaries, once human beings have lifted themselves above the level of cattle, then the 'basic', 'loftiest', and most 'sublime' idea of human existence becomes absolutely essential: belief in the immortality of the soul. Once this belief breaks down, as Dostoevsky saw in the nihilism or indifferentism of the Russian educated classes of the 1860s, then suicide is the only logical conclusion. Hence, Kirilov who has lost belief in the immortality of the soul is trying to write a book investigating the reasons why people do not kill themselves.

Thus, one might say that there is a path in the Continental tradition from the critique of Kant in Hamann and Jacobi, through to the religious and, indeed, irreligious anti-rationalism of Kierkegaard, Stirner, and Dostoevsky through to the post-war French existentialism of Sartre and Camus.

Unifying Kant's dualisms

The combined effect of the criticism of Kant's philosophy in the 1780s and 1790s was that the Enlightenment faith in reason seemed more questionable than ever. As Beiser remarks, 'Kant was not thwarting but abetting reason's self-destructive march towards the abyss.' It is obviously a separate issue as to whether this view of Kant is philosophically justified. The point is that an entire series of debates that define the Continental philosophical tradition take their leave from this point, and it is my contention that Continental philosophy has to be understood on this basis.

Let me conclude by returning to the earlier argument that Kant leaves us with a series of dualisms standing in need of unification. This is one of the objections presented by the philosopher that Kant regarded as his best critic: Salomon Maimon. Maimon's criticisms were published in 1790 as *Essay on Transcendental Philosophy*. His central argument is that the Kantian dualism between understanding and sensibility at the core of transcendental idealism is so drastic and deep that it prohibits the possibility of interaction between a priori concepts and empirical

7. Kant, mixing mustard in a pot. Drawing by Friedrich Hagemann (1801)

intuitions. This means that the argument of the transcendental deduction is invalidated by the very dualisms that Kant posits in order to carry out that deduction. This is what some Continental philosophers are fond of calling a 'performative self-contradiction'.

What it is important to see here is how Maimon's criticisms set the tone for post-Kantian philosophy. how do we overcome the pernicious dualisms of the Kantian system? What is required is some higher, unifying principle that would be immune to these criticisms. It is with this question that Fichte and German idealism begins. Fichte located this unifying principle in the activity of the subject. The dualism of theory and practice is unified in the self-reflection of the subject, its consciousness of freedom. This was the view that Fichte explored in the celebrated *The Doctrine of Science* (1794). For the young Schelling, on the contrary, the unifying principle was the notion of force or life, expressed in his early philosophy of nature. For Hegel, it was the notion of Spirit, for Arthur Schopenhauer it was the notion of the Will, for Nietzsche it was Power, for Marx it was Praxis, for Freud it was the Unconscious, for Heidegger it was Being. This list could be extended. The point here is that the problematic of Continental philosophy arose out of these criticisms of Kant and must be understood in this context.

Chapter 3

Spectacles and Eyes to See With: Two cultures in philosophy

It would not take a genius to realize that there are grave problems with the distinction between analytic and Continental philosophy. Continental philosophy is a highly eclectic and disparate series of intellectual currents that could hardly be said to amount to a unified tradition. As such, Continental philosophy is an *invention*, or, more accurately, a *projection* of the Anglo-American academy onto a Continental Europe that would not recognize the legitimacy of such an appellation – a little like asking for a Continental breakfast in Paris.

However, if the concept of Continental philosophy is taken at face value as a geographical category, then other problems arise. There are philosophers from the Continent, such as Frege and Carnap, who are not adjudged Continental, and philosophers from outside the Continent who are. Also, geographically, matters can become nicely confused, as when Dummett rightly claims that the term 'Anglo-American' (another toponym of no more obvious felicity than 'Continental') has done more harm than good because it elides the Germanophone origins of analytical philosophy. Dummett rather mischievously but accurately suggests in its place the term 'Anglo-Austrian'.

A more far-reaching objection to the distinction between analytic and Continental philosophy is that raised by Bernard Williams, when he claims that the distinction rests upon a confusion of geographical and methodological terms, as if one were to classify cars into front-wheel drive and Japanese. Although analytic philosophy is often powerfully associated with certain places, say Oxford or Princeton, it denotes a commitment to a certain method of philosophizing, to certain standards of argumentation, clarity, and rigour, whereas Continental philosophy would seem to denote a commitment to a certain place regardless of methodology. Thus, for Williams, the distinction between analytic and Continental philosophy rests upon a confused comparison of methodological and geographical categories.

However, such confusion would not be rectified by recasting the terms of the opposition into either strictly geographical (i.e. Anglo-American versus Continental) or methodological (i.e. analytic versus phenomenological) categories. If the opposition were recast geographically, then this would make matters even muddier, because it would wrongly imply both that philosophy in the UK, North America, and Australasia was by definition non-Continental, and that the founding father of analytic philosophy (Frege) and its greatest representative (Wittgenstein) were exclusively Continental philosophers. If the opposition is recast methodologically, then this would hardly begin to account for the fact that, on one side of the divide, very few philosophers can be said to engage in traditional forms of philosophical analysis (not to mention all talk of 'post-analytic' philosophy in recent years) and, on the other side, there is simply no category that would begin to cover the diversity of work produced by thinkers as methodologically and thematically opposed as Hegel and Kierkegaard, Freud and Martin Buber, Heidegger and Theodor Adorno, or Jacques Lacan and Deleuze.

Williams is rightly sceptical about any such drawing of distinctions between philosophical schools and doctrines because it disguises and disarms a more profound and interesting possible debate about the identity of philosophy itself. Although, in criticism of Williams, it is clear that for him the identity of philosophy is best represented by analytic philosophy, with its rather manly virtue of 'workmanlike truthfulness', which seems to be based upon a quite questionable analogy between philosophy and the procedures of the natural sciences, he clearly has a point here and I shall come back to this theme in the conclusion to this book. There is something ultimately parochial and intellectually cowardly about identifying oneself with either side of a perceived philosophical divide, because it prevents the possible intellectual challenges that would be the consequence of a dialogue outside of one's professional entrenchments.

A few lingering stereotypes

However, the distinction between analytic and Continental philosophy should not simply be pushed aside without an attempt to diagnose and exorcize some of the lingering cultural stereotypes within it. The professional entrenchments of philosophy continue to exist, and it is now a question of trying to find out why that is the case by looking at some choice examples.

Stanley Rosen, with his tongue firmly in his cheek, deftly summarizes the stereotypical representation of the distinction between analytic and Continental philosophy as follows: 'precision, conceptual clarity and systematic rigour are the property of analytical philosophy, whilst the continentals indulge in speculative metaphysics or cultural hermeneutics, or, alternatively, depending on one's sympathies, in wool-gathering and bathos'. Such stereotypes are, I fear, only confirmed by debates in the press and by the remarks of some professional philosophers who really should know better. For an example of the latter one need think no further than the Derrida affair in Cambridge in 1992, where certain prominent members of the University opposed Jacques Derrida's nomination for an honorary doctorate. On the day after the opposition had lost the vote, a quality British newspaper ran the headline 'Cognitive nihilism hits English city'.

But perhaps the gulf that separates the analytic and Continental traditions was most succinctly stated during the irritable and infamous discussion that followed Gilbert Ryle's paper at a conference on analytic philosophy in France in 1960, where in response to Maurice Merleau-Ponty's plea 'notre programme n'est-il pas le même? (is not our programme the same?)', Ryle answered, 'J'espère que non'. It is this 'I hope not', this steadfast 'no' in the face of the perceived exoticism of the Continent, that is so revealing of an ideological prejudice that surely should have no home in philosophy. This is the 'No. No. No.' of Baroness Thatcher's refusal of Jacques Delors' plans for European union that was the seed of her political downfall in 1990. The paradox here is that the young Ryle began his career as an exponent of phenomenology, his first publication was a strikingly thorough review of Heidegger's *Being and Time*, published in *Mind* in 1930, and he lectured extensively at Oxford in the 1930s on Bolzano, Brentano, Frege, Meinong, and Husserl. As Dummett understatedly intones, 'it is a great pity that little of his knowledge of those authors was preserved in print, and, equally, that, as far as I can see, little that he learned from them survived into his later work'.

Staying with Merleau-Ponty, A. J. Ayer eloquently demonstrates the gulf that separates analytic from Continental philosophers with the following reminiscence from his autobiography:

> it might have been expected that Merleau-Ponty and I should find some common ground for discussion. We did indeed attempt it on several occasions, but never got very far before we began to wrangle over some point of principle, on which neither of us would yield. Since these arguments tended to become acrimonious, we tacitly agreed to drop them and meet on a purely social level, which still left us quite enough to talk about.

This sounds a little like the shouting across the gulf of which Dummett speaks above. A further specimen, which also involves Ayer, is even more interesting, and even slightly improbable. It concerns a meeting between Ayer and perhaps the most excessive of Continental thinkers, Georges Bataille: anti-philosopher, un-knower, a-theologian, and eroticist. They met in a Parisian bar in 1951, with Merleau-Ponty. Apparently the discussion lasted until three in the morning, and the thesis under discussion was very simple: did the sun exist before the existence of human beings? Ayer saw no reason to doubt that it did, whereas Bataille thought the whole proposition meaningless. For a philosopher committed to a scientific view of the world, like Ayer, it makes sense to say that physical objects like the sun existed prior to the evolution of human beings. Whereas for Bataille, more versed in phenomenology, physical objects must be perceived from the position of a human subject in order to be said to exist. Given that no human beings existed at the time postulated in the proposition, it therefore makes no sense to claim that the sun existed prior to humans. Bataille concludes,

> I should say that yesterday's conversation produced an effect of shock. There exists between French and English philosophers a sort of abyss which we do not find between French and German philosophers.

For a revealing example of the lingering prejudice with which Continental philosophy is still treated, one might take as a case study a pair of articles by Lord Anthony Quinton on analytic and Continental philosophy respectively published in the *Oxford Companion to Philosophy* as recently as 1995. Quinton's piece on analytic philosophy is a fair summary of logical atomism and logical positivism, although it is too brief to be useful on post-war developments in the field. He concludes with reference to the analytic philosophers Hilary Putnam and Robert Nozick, 'they think and write in the analytic spirit, respectful of science, both as a paradigm of reasonable belief and in conformity with its argumentative rigour, its clarity, and its determination to be objective'. However, the same determination to be objective is not manifest in Quinton's companion article on Continental philosophy. The article begins, reasonably enough, with Quinton rightly pointing out how recently the current meaning was attached to Continental philosophy in Britain after the Second World War. Useful observations are also made on the unity of philosophical endeavour that characterized the Latin Middle Ages and the Renaissance, an admirably unproblematic dialogue between philosophers from Britain and the Continent that extended well into the Enlightenment, where Locke was a reader of Descartes, Gassendi, and Malebranche, Hume read Bayle and knew Rousseau, Mill studied Comte, etc. So far, so good. However, Quinton then goes on to claim that 'there is really no perceptible convergence between the two philosophical worlds', and as if (unintentionally, of course) to prove his point he provides quite shocking summaries of existentialism, structuralism, and critical theory: the first is rejected, without adequate reference to phenomenology, for its reliance 'on dramatic, even melodramatic, utterance rather than sustained rational argument'; the second is said to have 'culminated with Foucault and to have transcended itself, shooting off into outer intellectual space, with Derrida'; the third is bewilderingly dispatched in the following terms, 'The evident political intentions of the critical theorists ruled out any interest on the part of analytic philosophers, committed to neutrality'. If such comments can be said to exhibit a commitment to neutrality, not to mention the above-mentioned virtues of rigour, clarity, and a determination to be objective, then Quinton might very well be justified in his belief that there is no possible convergence between the two philosophical worlds. Needless to say, such remarks are not only incorrect, but, I believe, intellectually intolerant and simply serve to perpetuate pernicious cultural stereotypes.

Continental philosophy – professional self-description and cultural feature

How, then, do we explain this gulf between analytic and Continental philosophy and philosophers? The adjective 'Continental', at least for the British reader, evokes associations with other uses of the adjective, like a 'Continental breakfast' or what my mother used to call a 'Continental quilt'. That is to say, it is a geographical term or *toponym* that refers to something that occurs in a particular place, namely on the European Continent. The adjective opens up a distinction between the Continental and what is not Continental, a distinction that, from the British perspective, often risks hardening into an opposition between the British and the Continental, where the latter is defined as the foreign, the exotic, and the strange and the former as the homely, the native, and the familiar. As such, the notion of 'Continental' alludes to seemingly intractable and frankly rather tiresome issues of political geography, namely as to whether Britain is adrift from the Continent or the Continent is adrift from Britain (recall the infamous newspaper headline, 'Fog over the channel. Continent cut off').

Now, I want to make two claims about the historical meaning of Continental philosophy. First, it is essentially a *professional self-description*: that is, it is a way that philosophers and philosophy departments organize their research and teaching and indicate their intellectual allegiances. In this sense, Continental philosophy is a feature of the professionalization of philosophy. In this restricted sense, the notion of Continental philosophy is a recent coinage. Although there is no consensus on the precise origin of the concept of Continental philosophy as a professional self-description, it does not arise as a description of undergraduate and postgraduate courses in philosophy before the 1970s. It is clear that this happened in the USA before Britain, where the first postgraduate courses in Continental philosophy were offered at the universities of Essex and Warwick in the early 1980s. In the American context, and to a lesser extent in Britain, the term 'Continental philosophy' replaced the earlier formulations 'Phenomenology' or 'Phenomenology and Existential Philosophy'. These terms are preserved in the names of the professional associations most closely associated with Continental philosophy in the English-speaking world, the Society for Phenomenology and Existential

8. Peter Paul Rubens (1577–1640), 'The Four Philosophers'

Philosophy founded in 1962 and the British Society for Phenomenology founded in 1967. It would seem, then, that in the post-war period, Continental philosophy was broadly synonymous with phenomenology (often in an existential garb), a fact that is also reflected by certain introductory American book titles from the 1960s: *An Invitation to Phenomenology* (1965) and *Phenomenology in America* (1967). It is perhaps indicative that the latter title is both mimicked and transformed in 1983 with the appearance of *Continental Philosophy in America*. The reason why 'Phenomenology' is replaced with 'Continental philosophy' is not absolutely clear, but it would seem that it was introduced to take account of the various so-called post-structuralist Francophone movements of thought that were increasingly distant from and often hostile towards phenomenology: to a lesser extent the work of Jacques Lacan, Derrida, and Jean-François Lyotard, and to a greater extent Gilles Deleuze and Michel Foucault.

This de facto divide between analytic and Continental philosophy can be observed in sundry philosophical epiphenomena such as job descriptions asking for 'Continentalists' and in publishers' catalogues where special pages are given over to Continental philosophy, usually towards the back of the catalogue. As John Searle complacently asserts, there is a near-complete professional hegemony of analytic philosophy in the English-speaking world, where types of non-analytic philosophy, like phenomenology, feel it necessary to define their position in relation to this hegemony. However, despite this unquestionable hegemony, there are universities in the UK, Ireland, Canada, and Australia that specialize in Continental philosophy and many more in the USA, mostly amongst the Catholic universities, with some notable exceptions. In philosophy departments and faculties where the analytic tradition is dominant, there is often a course or paper on 'Modern European Philosophy', 'Post-Kantian Philosophy', or 'Phenomenology and Existentialism', courses that were often initiated as concessions to student demand, which is usually rather significant in this area. Also, the influence of Continental philosophy in the English-speaking world, particularly in its more recent Francophone versions, is arguably much stronger outside philosophy departments than within them, where it has decisively influenced many theoretical innovations in the humanities and social sciences: in literary theory, art history and theory, social and political theory, cultural studies, historiography, religious studies, and anthropology, not to mention debates in fine art, architecture, feminism, and psychoanalysis. Revealingly and significantly, the reception of Continental thought in the English-speaking world has, for the most part, taken place outside of philosophy departments.

However, if that were an end to the story, then discussions of Continental philosophy would be of as little general import as other professional disagreements within the humanities and the social sciences. To explain the persistent irritability of the disputes surrounding Continental philosophy revealed in Quinton's dismissiveness and Bataille's consternation, a second claim has to be made. Namely, that the notion of Continental philosophy as a professional self-description is more contested and corrosive because it overlays a more ancient *cultural* meaning, and goes back to debates about the relation of Britain and the English-speaking world to the European Continent, debates which are all too much alive in contemporary British politics, for example. In this sense, questions of the identity of a philosophical tradition become fatally enmeshed in the ideological prejudices of political geography, captured in vague and misleading notions such as 'British empiricism', 'French rationalism', 'German metaphysics', and so on.

The interesting case of John Stuart Mill

The intellectual history of the philosophical relation of Britain to the Continent goes back at least to the late 16th and 17th centuries, to the emergence of philosophy as something written in the vernacular, national languages like French and English, rather than in Latin. Convenient landmarks here are the publication of Montaigne's *Essais* in French in 1580 and Francis Bacon's *The Advancement of Learning* in English in 1605. But the key dimension that explains the emergence of something that one might identify as 'Continental philosophy' begins, I believe, a good deal later, with the reception of Kant and German idealism and romanticism in England in the years after the French revolution. The key figure here is the poet Samuel Taylor Coleridge and his influential, if idiosyncratic and irregular, understanding of German idealism and romanticism. Of enormous interest in this regard are two long essays by John Stuart Mill on Jeremy Bentham and Coleridge that appeared in the *London and Westminster Review* in 1832 and 1840 respectively. In connection with the German influences on Coleridge, Mill speaks of 'Continental philosophers' and 'the Continental philosophy'. He also speaks of 'the Germano-Coleridgean doctrine' and 'the French philosophy'. Early in the essay on Coleridge, Mill writes,

> Whoever could master the premises and combine the methods of both [Coleridge and Bentham] would possess the entire English philosophy of their age. Coleridge used to say that every one is born either a Platonist or an Aristotelian: it may be similarly affirmed, that every Englishman of the present day is by implication either a Benthamite or a Coleridgean; holds views of human affairs which can only be proved true on the principles either of Bentham or of Coleridge.

The interesting thought here is that the combination of Bentham and Coleridge gives one the entire English philosophy of the age. These twin tendencies are then ascribed with two questions: Mill thinks Bentham asks of any ancient doctrine or received opinion, '*Is it true?*'; whereas Coleridge asks, '*What is the meaning of it?*'. So, 'the Continental philosophy' is concerned with meaning, whereas its Benthamite opposite is concerned with truth. In terms of the schema of my opening chapter, if Bentham is concerned with the question of knowledge, then Coleridge is concerned with the question of wisdom.

Of course, it is extremely tempting to psychologize what Mill is saying here, for, in the winter of 1826-7, at the age of twenty, he underwent a severe 'mental crisis'. Mill asked himself, like many young people, whether he would be happy if all his objects in life were realized, and had to answer that he would not. The utilitarianism of Mill's extraordinary education produced knowledge but was inadequate for wisdom or, indeed, happiness. Mill partially overcame his depression through the reading of Wordsworth's poems, remarking, 'From them I seemed to learn what would be the perennial sources of happiness'. Mill learned, in his words, that 'I was not a stock or a stone', and was led to dissent from Bentham's judgement that 'poetry was no better than push-pin'. Mill decided it was a lot better than push-pin and immersed himself in the reading of the Coleridgeans, and their German predecessors, such as Goethe, whose 'many-sidedness' Mill admired, and the humanistic philosopher and linguist, Wilhelm von Humboldt. When asked by the historian Thomas Carlyle whether he had entirely changed his opinion of matters, Mill replied, referring to the logic on which he had been brought up, 'I believe in spectacles', but added, 'but I think eyes are necessary too'.

Returning to Mill's two essays, Bentham is the great 'subversive' or 'in the language of continental philosophers, the great critical thinker of his age and country'. Such subversive critique proceeds by using methods of logical analysis and empirical good sense to ask after the truth of 'things practical'. For Mill, Bentham is a sort of practically minded extension of Humean scepticism carried over in particular into the areas of law and government. To his great credit, Bentham used these critical gifts in a socially reformist spirit, to improve the common weal. Coleridge, on the other hand, was not concerned with asking after the truth of things, but after their meaning. As such, the method is not destructive of received doctrine and tradition, but

9. Caricature of John Stuart Mill (1806–73)

rather offers a hermeneutic reconstruction of the meaning of such doctrines and traditions. In contemporary terms, thinking of the influential work of Quentin Skinner, one would call this a 'contextualist' approach to matters. That is, if we want to *understand* the meaning of a specific practice, event, or indeed text then we have to reconstruct its historical emergence and place it in the complex web of social and political life. In this sense, surprisingly perhaps, it is 'the Coleridgean-Continental philosophy' that is conservative of tradition and the great enemy of social upheaval, whereas it is Bentham who is destructive of tradition and the friend of social change and progress. One is used to thinking of the distinction between traditions or tendencies the other way round, where analytic philosophy is conservative and stuffy in a sort of senior common room, leather arm-patch sort of a way, and Continental philosophy is its funky, streetwise, leather-jacketed obverse. Interestingly, we shall have occasion to meet an analogous political division in the conflict between Carnap and Heidegger, where the former is reformist and progessive, whereas the latter, at his worst, is reactionary and conservative.

We might schematize some of the oppositions gleaned from Mill in the following way:

Bentham	Coleridge
truth	meaning
critically destructive	hermeneutically reconstructive
social change, reform	social conservatism
progress	tradition
(analytic)	(continental)

Seen in this way, the distinction between analytic and Continental philosophy is not a geographical distinction between different places, like Britain and the Continent, but is rather a difference that is internal to what might be called 'the English philosophical mind'. Otherwise put, it

45

is a difference that is native to a specific culture, a culture that is therefore internally divided and thoroughly sectarian. Mill puts the point eloquently, comparing philosophical conflict with religious intolerance.

> The spirit of philosophy in England, like that of religion, is still rootedly sectarian. Conservative thinkers and Liberals, transcendentalists and admirers of Hobbes and Locke, regard each other as out of the pale of philosophical discourse; look upon each other's speculations as vitiated by an original taint, which makes all study of them, except for purposes of attack, useless if not mischievous.

Although written over a hundred and fifty years ago, this might well be a description of the way in which many philosophers view their professional enemies from across the gulf – or departmental corridor – that separates them. Professional philosophy risks being as sectarian as a religious conflict where one only studies one's enemy in the preparation for attack. But let us not dwell too long on such nasty details.

What, then, is to be done? Mill makes the following interesting suggestion.

> For, among the truths long recognized by Continental philosophers, but which very few Englishmen have yet arrived at, one is the importance, in the present imperfect state of mental and social science, of antagonist modes of thought: which are as necessary to one another in speculation, as mutually checking powers are in a political constitution. A clear insight, indeed, into this necessity is the only rational or enduring basis of philosophical tolerance . . .

Mill goes on to add that the great danger in things philosophical,

> is not so much of embracing falsehood for the truth, as of mistaking part of the truth for the whole. It might plausibly be maintained that in almost every one of the leading controversies, past or present, in social

philosophy, both sides were in the right in what they affirmed, though wrong in what they denied; and that if either could have been made to take the other's view in addition to its own, little more would have been needed to make its doctrine correct.

A number of strands can be picked out from this passage. First, a truth common to 'the Continental philosophy' is the necessity for antagonistic modes of thought. Namely, that the truth is not to be found in any part of the whole, but through the reflection on the whole as such. Although Mill makes no mention of Hegel, this is a very Hegelian thought, close to Hegel's notion of 'dialectics'. In the preface to the *Phenomenology of Spirit*, Hegel writes 'the true is the whole', meaning by this that if one is to attain real wisdom and knowledge in things philosophical (what Hegel calls 'Absolute Knowing'), then one must view the vast variety of theses and positions that make up the history and present of philosophy as each expressing a grain of truth. To pick one grain from the pile is to risk missing out on the rich bread that one can bake from a whole batch of grain.

Mill compares the need for such antagonism or dialectics with the checks and balances that are an essential part of a liberal and democratic system of government. One justification for a competitive party system in government is that it is the duty of the opposition to continually examine the policy and legislation of the party of government, and vice versa when the roles are reversed, as they must be. In Mill's hopeful view, then, the error in philosophy is mistaking part of the truth for the whole, or, as Hegel puts it, of placing fear of error higher than the desire for truth. In this sense, it is not a question of deciding whether Bentham or Coleridge is right, but in seeing both philosophical tendencies as the combined expression of a larger truth – namely that human beings are concerned by questions of both knowledge and wisdom – they require both spectacles to look through and eyes to see with. Philosophy requires both critical and logical destruction and patient hermeneutic reconstruction. That is, analytic and Continental philosophy are two halves of a larger cultural whole, and the truth in things philosophical will not be attained by affirming one side and denying the other, but as Mill says 'by taking the other's view in addition to its own'.

Two cultures in philosophy

In summary, I have made two historical claims for Continental philosophy: it is a professional self-description and it is a cultural feature. As a self-description, Continental philosophy is a necessary – but perhaps transitory – evil of the professionalization of the discipline. As a cultural feature, Continental philosophy goes back at least to the time of Mill, and what can be learned from his views is that the division between philosophical traditions is the expression of a conflict (and moreover a sectarian conflict) that is internal to 'Englishness' and not a geographical opposition between the English-speaking world and the Continent. As such, the gulf between analytic and Continental philosophy is the expression of a deep cultural divide between differing and opposed habits of thought – let's call them Benthamite and Coleridgean, or empirical–scientific and hermeneutic–romantic. Mill's deeper point is that the philosophical and cultural truth of matters, whatever that might be, is not to be found by choosing sides, and thereby mistaking a part for the whole. Rather, in Hegel's words, the true is the whole, and the whole has to be understood in its systematic movement and historical development. This book is hopefully a contribution to such understanding.

It is my belief that much of the hostility and suspicion shown by analytic philosophers to Continental philosophy takes place because these two claims – professional and cultural – are unhelpfully conflated and sides are chosen. But this hostility is not always one-sided. In addition to the Benthamite beastliness of some analytic philosophers, it might also be said to arise from the Coleridgean lunacy of some Continental philosophers, when they fail to grasp the conditions of their cultural location and speak the language of the tribe. For example, Heidegger and Derrida are great philosophers, but there is absolutely no point writing like them in English. The results are, at best, embarrassingly derivative and, at worst, unintelligible. What Continental philosophers have to understand, then, is the 'Englishness' of Continental philosophy. Although I cannot go into it here, I think that similar remarks might be made about the 'American-ness', 'Australasian-ness', 'Canadian-ness', or whatever, of Continental philosophy in the English-speaking world.

In other words, there are two cultures in philosophy, and little will change in philosophy, or indeed in culture, until this situation is adequately reflected upon. Nearly a hundred and twenty years after the publication of Mill's essay on Coleridge, on 7 May 1959, C. P. Snow gave the famous Rede Lecture in the Senate House in Cambridge. In it he diagnosed the loss of a common culture and the emergence of two distinct cultures: those represented by scientists on the one hand and those Snow termed 'literary intellectuals' on the other. If the former are in favour of social reform and progress through science, technology, and industry, then intellectuals are what Snow terms 'natural Luddites' in their understanding of and sympathy for advanced industrial society. In Mill's terms, the division is between Benthamites and Coleridgeans. In 'The Two Cultures: A Second Look' (1963), written after years of the sometimes vicious controversy to which the 1959 lecture gave rise, Snow offered the following précis of his main argument in his impeccably spare prose style:

> In our society (that is, advanced western society) we have lost even the pretence of a common culture. Persons educated with the greatest intensity we know can no longer communicate with each other on the plane of their major intellectual concern. This is serious for our creative, intellectual and, above all, normal life. It is leading us to interpret the past wrongly, to misjudge the present, and to deny our hopes of

the future. It is making it difficult or impossible for us to take good action.

I gave the most pointed example of this lack of communication in the shape of two groups of people, representing what I have christened 'the two cultures'. One of these contained the scientists, whose weight, achievement and influence did not need stressing. The other contained the literary intellectuals. I did not mean that literary intellectuals act as the main decision makers of the western world. I meant that literary intellectuals vocalise, and to some extent shape and predict the mood of the non-scientific culture: they do not make the decisions, but their words seep into the minds of those who do. Between these two groups – the scientists and the literary intellectuals – there is little communication and, instead of fellow-feeling, something like hostility.

This was intended as a description of, or a very crude first approximation to, our existing state of affairs. That it was a state of affairs I passionately disliked, I thought was made fairly clear.

The resonance here with Mill's remarks is clear, particularly the hostility felt by respective representatives of the two cultures towards each other. As with Mill, it is tempting to psychologize Snow's effort. He had obtained a First in Chemistry in 1927 and in 1928 began a Ph.D. at Cambridge, working at the world-famous Cavendish Laboratory headed by Lord Rutherford. He went on to be a distinguished research scientist and in 1964 became second-in-command in Harold Wilson's newly established Ministry of Technology. However, he had always had a passion for literature, and in 1932 published a detective story, *Death Under Sail*, which was followed by no less than eleven novels in the 'Strangers and Brothers' series, which were immensely popular. So, in many ways, his expression of the crisis of the two cultures was a *cri de coeur*. However, as with Mill, it was also part of a wider cultural pathology.

Snow was subjected to a vicious *ad hominem* attack by the leading literary and cultural critic of the time, F. R. Leavis, who complained of 'Snow's panoptic pseudo-cogencies' and lack of literary understanding. Such elitist nose-holding was rightly ignored by Snow, but it is clear that what was being played out in the Snow–Leavis debate was the by now familiar conflict of Bentham versus Coleridge, utilitarian versus romantic. Indeed, this is a familiar clash in English cultural history. As a final example, historically in the middle between Mill and Snow, there is the dispute between T. H. Huxley and Matthew Arnold. In brief, Huxley argued in an 1880 lecture, given in Birmingham, then the industrial hub of Britain, for a scientific education against the prevailing classical canon that dominated the universities. Arnold responded in the 1882 Rede Lecture in Cambridge, 'Literature and Science', by claiming that both literature and science could be integrated into a wider, more Germanic, understanding of science as *Wissenschaft*, of knowledge in the broad sense. Although a constructive response, the proof of the pudding was found in Arnold's steadfast opposition to revising the classicism of the university canon. So the story goes on, and other more contemporary examples could doubtless be added.

So, my suggestion is that we would do well to understand the current divisions in philosophy in terms of a two-cultures model, where it is the clash between the poles of this antagonism that constitutes what we think of as culture. As such, it is extremely unlikely that either or both of these two poles will disappear. As Mill says, there is a truth to antagonism which 'the Continental philosophers' have known about for some time. The best that can be hoped for is that the parties of this antagonism at least come to the view that the other's existence is legitimate and that there might be something to be talked about and, at best, learned from the other side.

Snow's answer to this philosophical and cultural divide is very simple and can be summarized in one word: *education*. In my view, he is still right. The cultural pathology offered by Snow fed, more or less directly, into the Robbins Report on Higher Education in 1963 and to the founding of a number of 'new universities': Sussex, Warwick, York, Keele, Kent, East Anglia, and my own, Essex. The implicit brief of these universities was to address the two-cultures problem by insisting that students have a broad education, where natural scientists should study topics in the humanities and social sciences, and vice versa. It is a depressing fact that as a consequence of the attack on the universities initiated by Thatcher's government in the early 1980s, this mission has been largely abandoned by these institutions, and what has taken its place is the vague talisman of 'interdisciplinarity'.

As a final thought, we might consider Stephen Toulmin's argument in *Cosmopolis*, where he boldly argues there are two cultures because there were two beginnings to modernity, one humanistic, the other rationalistic. If the name of Descartes is habitually associated with the latter, then it is Toulmin's contention that the scientific modernity that begins in the early decades of the 17th century obscures and even distorts a humanistic modernity that can be indexed to the practically minded humanistic scepticism of Montaigne's *Essais* that appeared in 1580. There has been, for Toulmin, an unrecognized twin trajectory of modernity – humanistic and scientific – which has led to the breakdown or breaking apart of the integrity of theory and practice, truth and meaning, or knowledge and wisdom. Toulmin's optimistic suggestion (too optimistic to my mind, but admirable nonetheless) is that we need to humanize modernity and to do this we require a rebirth of practical philosophy. Wittgenstein's later writings reactivate the humanistic scepticism of Montaigne and renew the practical impulse to philosophize. Toulmin writes:

> If the Two Cultures are still estranged, then, this is no local peculiarity of 20th-century Britain: it is a reminder that Modernity had two distinct starting points, a humanistic one grounded in classical literature, and a scientific one rooted in 17th Century natural philosophy.

What has yet to be explained is why these two traditions were not seen from the beginning as complementary, rather than in competition. Whatever was gained by Galileo, Descartes and Newton's excursions into natural philosophy, something was also lost through the abandonment of Erasmus and Rabelais, Shakespeare and Montaigne.

Spectacles and Eyes to See With

Chapter 4

Can Philosophy Change the World? Critique, praxis, emancipation

Nothing seems to me less outdated than the classical emancipatory ideal.

Jacques Derrida

Having presented in the last two chapters some sort of historical account of Continental philosophy, let me now try and develop a more systematic account of the differences with analytic philosophy. This will lead on to the crucial role of tradition, history, and what is called 'historicity'. I will end the chapter by proposing a particular model of philosophical practice based around three terms: *critique, praxis*, and *emancipation*. This cluster of concepts will hopefully begin to explain why so much philosophy in the Continental tradition is concerned with giving a philosophical critique of the social practices of the modern world that aspires towards a notion of individual or societal emancipation. In other words, much Continental philosophy asks us to look at the world critically with the intention of identifying some sort of transformation, whether personal or collective. In my view, it is this set of background assumptions that connects classical philosophers like Hegel and Nietzsche with their contemporary heirs like Jürgen Habermas, Foucault, and Derrida.

Proper names or problems?

Richard Rorty is one of the few English-speaking philosophers who has consistently and heroically attempted to blur the distinction between analytic and Continental philosophy by working with a foot in both camps. He has consequently and unjustifiably been shot at by both sides for getting it wrong. Rorty has tended to root both analytic and Continental traditions in the American pragmatism of John Dewey. Rorty suggests that the distinction between traditions essentially consists in the fact that analytic philosophy deals with problems, whereas Continental philosophy deals with proper names. Now, this would seem to be more or less right insofar as Continental philosophy is habitually presented by people like me as a roughly chronological sequence of proper names beginning with Kant, rather than the problem-orientated approach that one tends to associate with the tradition of analytic philosophy. But one must be cautious here because Rorty's criterion for distinguishing between traditions might be said to be something of a generalization that confirms the ridiculous stereotype that the Continental tradition is somehow unconcerned with problems and their argumentation.

Yet Rorty's remark does capture something interesting, insofar as books, papers, and discussions in contemporary Continental philosophy, both on the Continent and in the English-speaking world, have a tendency to focus around the texts of a particular canonical philosopher, or offer a comparative study of the texts of two or more philosophers. Thus, rather than writing a paper called 'The Concept of Truth', one might write a paper on 'The Concept of Truth in Husserl and Heidegger'; rather than writing a paper on 'The Communitarian Critique of Liberalism', one might write on 'The Relevance of Hegel's critique of Kant for Contemporary Political Theory'; rather than write on 'The Limits of Ethical Theory', one might write on 'The Eternal Return of Nietzsche's Genealogical Critique of Morality'; rather than write on 'The Problem of Personal Identity', one might write on 'The Concept of the Subject from Kant to Derrida'; and so on.

It is fair to say that this practice often mystifies and infuriates philosophers trained in the analytic tradition, who maintain that Continental philosophers are only doing commentary and not original thinking: this is mere Frenchified *explication de texte* and not rigorous philosophical argumentation. It is arguable that there is too great a propensity towards commentary to the detriment of originality in contemporary Continental philosophy in the English-speaking world. But what is lacking in such a criticism (and in Rorty's criterion) is the recognition of a distinct practice of philosophy with a quite different sense of the importance of translation, commentary, interpretation, tradition, and history for contemporary philosophical research. It is not that philosophy in the Continental tradition is dismissive of problems – far from it – it is rather that problems are often approached *textually and contextually*, and therefore demand a different mode of treatment, one that might *appear* more indirect.

Texts and contexts

Stanley Cavell is another major American philosopher who has consistently refused to allow his work to be pigeon-holed into either analytic or Continental styles of thinking. However, unlike Rorty, Cavell roots both traditions back into the philosophically neglected tradition of American transcendentalism, whose definitive expression is found in the work of Ralph Waldo Emerson and Henry David Thoreau. Cavell writes at the beginning of his magnum opus, *The Claim of Reason* (1979), 'I have wished to understand philosophy not as a set of problems but as a set of texts'. However, I think this puts the point too strongly. I would contend, rather, that the various intellectual traditions that have shaped contemporary Continental philosophy constitute a determinate but ever-reconfiguring constellation of texts, a sort of star-cluster of texts where some will shine more brightly for a while and then fade, at which point our attention is drawn by the light of other stars. Some of these texts will swell like Red Giants to absorb everything else in their field, whereas others will shrink like Black Holes and fail to emit any light. As we all know, the way in which the night sky appears is determined by our place on the globe, and the intensity with which certain texts will burn depends on the context from which they are seen and other contingent factors, like the amount of intellectual pollution in the atmosphere.

To choose a more prosaic image, the texts of the Continental tradition make up a kind of documentary archive of philosophical problems, with a distinct relation to their context and our own and marked by a strong consciousness of history. We will use different resources in this archive at different times, depending on the nature of the problems we are confronted with and seeking to think through. But what characterizes many of the texts in this archive is that – like those of Hegel, Marx, and Nietzsche – they are characterized by a strong historical self-consciousness that will not allow them to be read without reference to their context or our own. It is such a historical approach that I took in Chapters 2 and 3, where I sought to establish the philosophical problematic of post-Kantian thought by reconstructing the textual and contextual history of that period in the German-speaking world and the conditions for its reception in the English-speaking world. Such an approach not only has the considerable virtue of making the history of philosophy into a good read that one may want to find out more about, but it also implies that systematic philosophical argument cannot be divorced from the textual and contextual conditions of its historical emergence.

Let me give four recent examples of this:

1   The interest in Kant's *Critique of Judgement* in the 1980s and in particular in the discussion of the concept of the sublime was both the cause and the consequence of the problems posed by the

modernity/postmodernity debate. As such, the often acrimonious exchanges as to whether modernity was over (the position of Jean-François Lyotard) or simply incomplete (the position of Habermas) turned on how one read Kant and where one chose to place the emphasis in one's reading. Happily, that debate has become rather stale and the discussion has moved on.

2   When I was an undergraduate in philosophy during the early 1980s, Schelling was a name we had either not heard or heard only in connection with Hegel's early critique of his work. The recent growth of interest in Schelling arose out of perceived philosophical problems in the Anglo-American reception of French 'post-structuralist' thought. It became clear that the shape of argument in a thinker like Derrida bore striking similarities to that of Schelling, and if that was the case then perhaps 'deconstruction' was not quite so avant-garde as had previously been imagined.

3   Emmanuel Levinas is now generally considered one of the greatest French philosophers of the 20th century. Yet, his work was largely ignored in France until the mid-1980s. The current flood of work on Levinas seems to have been the direct consequence of 'the Heidegger affair' in the winter of 1986–7, when the extent of Heidegger's shameful involvement in Nazism became clear. So, the interest in Levinas arises in the context of the ethical and political myopia of Heidegger's thinking and, by implication, in the thinking which Heidegger inspired, notably Derrida's deconstruction.

4   With the notable exception of the pioneering work of Charles Taylor, Hegel was until fairly recently a rather shadowy figure in the Anglo-American philosophical canon. The current renewal of interest in the work of Hegel is the consequence of debates in contemporary Anglo-American philosophy in the works of John McDowell, Robert Brandom, and others about the limitations of naturalism in philosophy and the need to find a way of harmonizing nature with freedom or reason.

Other examples of the kind could be given, where the Continental tradition functions as a kind of vast textual archive for contextually specific philosophical problems. A substantive contemporary philosophical problem will lead one to recall a text and a cluster of concepts from that archive. The way one moves forward philosophically is by looking backwards in a fresh manner.

In other words, for the Continental tradition, philosophical problems do not fall from the sky ready-made and cannot be treated as elements in some ahistorical fantasy of *philosophia perennis*. One's reading of a classic philosophical text from the tradition does not so much take the form of a college dinner conversation, as much as a meeting with a stranger from a distant land whose language one is only beginning to understand, and with difficulty. I remember, with no little embarrassment, giving a paper to some philosophers at a major British university a little after the beginning of my academic career. Over dinner, after enduring my long disquisition on the changing meaning of the concept of the subject from Aristotle to Descartes to Heidegger to Derrida, I was asked over dinner, 'why can't I read Descartes as if I were having dinner with him, just like I am having dinner with you?' I responded that Descartes died 350 years ago, after seeing at first hand the utter chaos of the Thirty Years War, that he wrote in Latin and French, and that he employed particular literary genres like the autobiographical essay *(Discourse on the Method)* and the spiritual exercise *(Meditations on First Philosophy)*. Therefore, I concluded, one cannot simply read through those factors to decide whether his arguments are valid or not. Needless to say, I failed to convince my interlocutor and the other guests at dinner, but the scene is instructive nonetheless in differences of philosophical approach.

That is, philosophical problems are textually and contextually *embedded* and, simultaneously, *distanced*. It is this combination of embeddedness and distance which perhaps explains why seemingly peripheral problems of translation, language, reading, text-reception, interpretation, and the hermeneutic access to history are of such central importance in the Continental tradition. Of course, this often leaves one open to the bewildering charge that one is doing 'literature' rather than 'philosophy'. As if a philosopher's propositions had some unmediated and transparent relation to experience, a desire which seems to be modelled upon what Wilfrid Sellars called 'The myth of the given', namely the idea that philosophical knowledge is straightforwardly and self-evidently founded on objects with which we are directly acquainted or are 'immediately before the mind'.

Tradition and history

Thus, although insufficient as a criterion, to identify the distinction between traditions in terms of a superficial difference between proper names and problems leads on to deeper questions of tradition and history, and the centrality of the latter for the Continental tradition. Perhaps the easiest and most concise way to characterize the distinction between analytic and Continental philosophy is in terms of what each sees as the shape of its tradition and which philosophers constitute that tradition. That is to say, what matters here is which tradition the philosopher *feels* part of, knowing who counts (and perhaps more importantly, knowing who doesn't count – sometimes without knowing why) as an ancestor or an authority. Thus, whereas an analytic philosopher might cite Frege, Russell, and G. E. Moore as ancestral authorities, a Continental philosopher might cite Hegel, Husserl, and Heidegger. In this sense, both analytic and Continental philosophy might be identified through their ancestral clusters, like old family portraits and photographs where one can detect resemblances between those ancient faces and their present-day heirs.

But making the distinction in this way does not really get to the nub of the issue, because what is curious about analytic philosophy, from a Continental perspective, is that, until pretty recently, it has been singularly unselfconscious about its tradition. This is beginning to change and interesting work has been done on the origins of analytic philosophy, whether in relation to its Germanophone roots in Frege, as we have already seen in the case of Dummett, or in relation to Russell's critique of British idealism. The emergence of analytic philosophy in the early decades of the 20th century can be seen as running in parallel with wider modernist movements in poetry, fine art, and architecture. With this in mind, it is perhaps not so surprising that Wittgenstein was not only the author of the *Tractatus Logico-Philosophicus*, but also designed and built a house in the most austere modernist style for his sister in Vienna.

Another significant symptom the recent 'historicization' of analytic philosophy has been the emergence of biography as a matter of legitimate philosophical interest and great cultural curiosity. The prime example here, once again, is Wittgenstein, in Ray Monk's wonderful book *Ludwig Wittgenstein. The Duty of Genius* (1990), and in Derek Jarman's slightly less wonderful film, *Wittgenstein* (1993). This biographical turn has been reinforced by Monk's 1996 biography of Bertrand Russell, and by successful recent biographies of Isaiah Berlin and A. J. Ayer. On the Continental side, Rüdiger Safranski's intellectual biography of Heidegger is worthy of mention. The lure of biography is that a philosopher's intellectual production can be seen as the expression of a specific existential attitude. As such – and this is the particular seduction of Wittgenstein – philosophy can be seen to be embodied in a way of life. Thus, to endorse or champion the views of a particular philosopher might lead to a certain mimicking or attempted emulation of that life. One sees this all the time professionally, where the students of a charismatic and famous philosopher will not only defend his or her doctrine, but also imitate their hand gestures, hesitations, verbal tics, and even their smoking, drinking, and sexual habits. Discipleship is not too strong a word for what is taking place here. But this is hardly a new idea, as biography was a central tool in philosophical instruction in the ancient world, obviously with the example of Socrates, but also in the various later Hellenistic schools, like the Stoics and Epicureans. In biography, a philosophy fuses with a way of life.

Historicity and emancipation

Staying with the question of history, I take it that much of the Continental tradition would refuse the validity of the distinction between philosophy and the history of philosophy operative in much of the analytic tradition. This is also why the focus on the post-Kantian tradition is so important for Continental philosophy, because, with the notable exception of Giambattista Vico and the later example of Jean-Jacques Rousseau, it is here that the question of history becomes philosophically central in the work of Hamann, Herder, and most of all in Hegel. One might say that the gain of the Continental tradition is that it allows one to focus on the essentially historical nature of philosophy as a practice and the essentially historical nature of the philosopher who engages in this practice. This is the insight into what is usually called 'historicity'.

This insight into historicity has the consequence that deep philosophical questions about the meaning and value of human life can no longer legitimately be referred to the traditional topics of speculative metaphysics – God, freedom, and immortality – topics regarded as cognitively meaningless, although morally defensible, by Kant. Rather, the recognition of the essential historicity of philosophy (and philosophers) implies two matters:

1   the radical *finitude* of the human subject, i.e. that there is no God-like standpoint or point of reference outside of human experience from which our experience might be characterized and judged; or, if there is, then we can know nothing about it
2   the thoroughly *contingent* or *created* character of human experience. That is, human experience is all-too-human, it is made

10. Hegel writing the *Phenomenology of Spirit*, oblivious to the battle of Jena raging outside his window, 14 October 1806. Drawing by Phillips Ward

and remade by us, and the circumstances of this fabrication are by definition contingent.

Once the human being has been located as a finite subject embedded in an ultimately contingent network of history, culture, and society, then one can begin to understand a feature common to many philosophers in the Continental tradition, namely the demand that things be otherwise. If human experience is a contingent creation, then it can be recreated in other ways. This is the demand for a transformative practice of philosophy, art, poetry, or thinking that would be capable of addressing, criticizing, and ultimately redeeming the present. The demand, then, that runs through much Continental thought and which continues to inspire philosophers like Habermas and Derrida, is that human beings *emancipate* themselves from their current conditions, which are conditions not amenable to freedom. As Rousseau said – and this was the rallying cry of the young German and English romantics at the end of the 18th century – 'Man was born free, but is everywhere in chains.' Critique and emancipation are two ends of the same piece of string.

The most dramatic statement of the link between critique and emancipation I know of can be found in a strange and wonderfully naive form in a short text, scribed on both sides of a single folio sheet, which probably dates from the summer of 1796: the so-called 'Oldest System-Programme of German Idealism' (see the Appendix on pp. 129–31). Philological study has established that the text was written in the hand of the young Hegel, although the ideas expressed reflect more closely those of the young Schelling and, to a lesser extent, the great German poet Johann Christoph Friedrich Hölderlin. Indeed, some years earlier, the three of them had studied together at the theological seminary in Tübingen, southern Germany. Schelling would go on to be appointed to a professorship in Jena in 1798 at the astonishingly tender age of 23. The 'System-Programme' has a peculiar history. Although its existence was known of by the editors of Hegel's unpublished work, Förster and

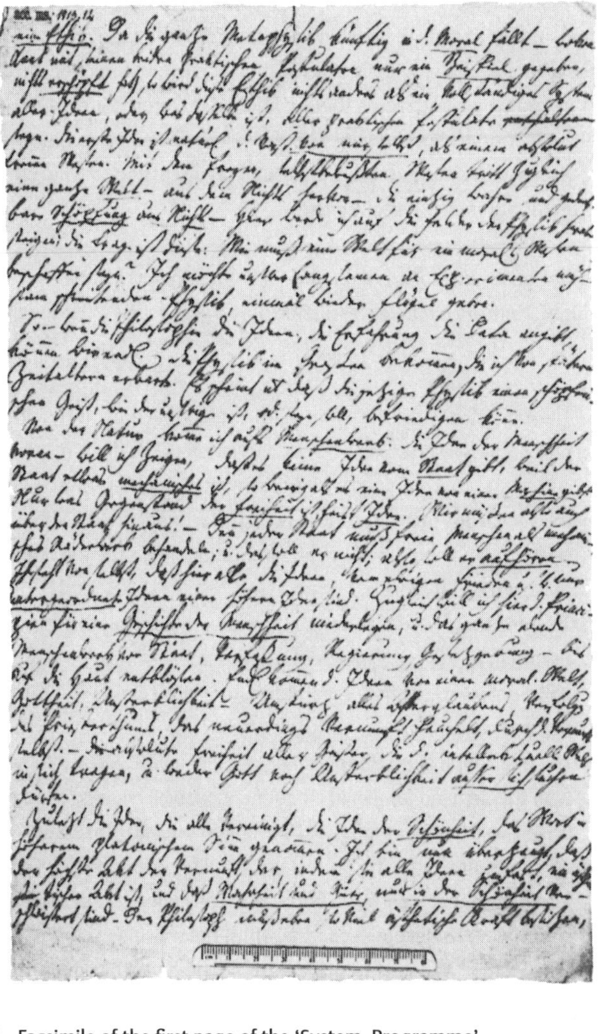

11. Facsimile of the first page of the 'System-Programme'

Boumann, it was not included in their 1834–5 collection of miscellaneous Hegelian writings, probably because the text did not harmonize well with the more conservative views of the mature Hegel. The 'System-Programme' was one of the last of Hegel's texts to be offered up for auction in Berlin in 1913, when it was bought by the Prussian State Library. The first publication and commentary of the text was in 1917 when it attracted the attention of the great German-Jewish philosopher, Franz Rosenzweig, who gave the text its now famous title and who initiated the extensive philosophical discussion to which the 'System-Programme' has given rise.

The text neatly crystallizes a number of themes in post-Kantian thought. Here are eight key discussion points that it raises, but there are others.

1   The idea (that we already met in Chapter 2) that what is required philosophically after Kant is a reconciliation of the dualisms of critical system combined with the romantic idea that the artwork is the vehicle for such a reconciliation. The artwork provides a sensuous image of freedom, and brings into harmony the domains of nature and reason.

2   The idea that in order to create this artwork the philosopher must become like the poet, and possess the same aesthetic power. Philosophy and poetry – separated since Plato's *Republic* – must become one.

3   The unification of philosophy and poetry in an artwork is of a piece with the demand for a *mythology of reason*, which would allow the people to become rational and the philosophers to become sensuous. At this point, 'eternal unity will reign among us'. The idea here is that in order to become socially effective, the ideas of reason have to become concrete. Thus, the way in which the formalism of Kantian rationality is to be avoided is by embodying reason in the form of myth. This is what is also called in the text 'a sensuous religion'.

4   The mythology of reason then functions as what we might call an ideology in politics, an ideology that is both critical and emancipatory.

5   It is critical because in order to achieve freedom we have to destroy what stands in the way of freedom, which in the text is identified as the mechanism of the state, which treats free people like machines. Therefore, apocalyptically stated, 'it must come to an end'. This destruction of the state also implies the elimination of the state religion, characterized by the 'despising gaze', where free people tremble 'before its wise men and priests'.

6   It is emancipatory because the goal of the mythology of reason is the achievement of a new organization of society based on freedom and equality: 'Only then can we expect the *same* development of *all* powers.'

7   So, it is through the creative power of art in the form of a mythology of reason that we can intimate the dimensions of a politically transformed life. This reveals what we might call the 'Rousseauism' of early German idealism and romanticism, which wanted to establish a new form of moral sociality, with freedom and equality between all men and women. For the romantics in particular, in England as well as Germany, this meant a society based on friendship, where all friends would be free and equal.

8   So, in the wonderfully naive utopianism of this once forgotten fragment, one sees the inspiration of Kant's critique of metaphysics blend together with the emancipatory spirit of the 1789 French Revolution into an aesthetic manifesto where 'truth and goodness are brothers only in beauty'. As the great Marxist critic Georg Lukács said of the Jena romantics, 'It was a dance on a glowing volcano, it was a radiantly improbable dream'. True enough, it was utterly improbable, but it is still radiant.

12. Eugène Delacroix (1798–1863), 'Liberty Leading the People',
28 July 1830

An appeal to tradition that is in no way traditional

So, Continental philosophy is inseparable from a relation to its tradition.
Indeed, this is a thought that we have already encountered in Mill's
categorization of Bentham and Coleridge in terms of the distinction
between progessive and traditional. But Mill is far too hasty in his
association of tradition with conservatism. It is indeed true that a
relation to tradition can be socially conservative, as in the mature
Coleridge or in the classical political conservatism of Edmund Burke.
However, the appeal to tradition need not at all be traditional, insofar as
what the notion of tradition is attempting to recover is something
missing, forgotten, or repressed in contemporary life. As such, the
appeal to tradition need not be some conservative acquiescence in the
face of the past, but can rather take the form of a *critical* confrontation
with the history of philosophy and history as such. Such a critical

conception of tradition is what Heidegger calls the *Destruktion* (de-structuring) or *Abbau* (dismantling) of the history of metaphysics, words that the young Derrida sought to render into French as *déconstruction*. The controversial concept of deconstruction should be approached uncontroversially, then, and thought of as an attempted critical dismantling of the tradition in terms of what has been unthought within it and what remains to be thought by it. In this sense, one can speak of a *radical* experience of tradition. Let me try and make this a little more concrete by turning to two notable ways of thinking of tradition radically, those of Husserl and his most celebrated student, Heidegger.

Tradition can be said to have two senses.

1 As something inherited or handed down without questioning or critical interrogation. This is the conservative concept of tradition Mill speaks of in relation to Coleridge.
2 As something made or produced through a critical engagement with the first sense of tradition, as an appeal to tradition that is in no way traditional, a radical tradition.

It is this second sense of tradition that is shared – not without some substantial differences, but that is another story – by Husserl and Heidegger. For the later Husserl of the posthumously published *Crisis of the European Sciences* (1954), the two senses of tradition correspond to the distinction between a *sedimented* and a *reactivated* experience of tradition. It is helpful to think of sedimentation in geological terms as a process of settling or consolidation. For Husserl, sedimentation consists in the forgetfulness of the origin of a state of affairs. Let me take up Husserl's celebrated example of geometry, which appears in the 1936 essay, 'The Origin of Geometry', published as an appendix to the *Crisis*. It should not be forgotten that this essay was the subject matter of Derrida's first book, which was simply a translation of and commentary upon Husserl's essay. Simply stated, Husserl's central argument is that if

13. Portrait of Edmund Husserl (1859–1938) as a student

the origin of geometry is forgotten, then one forgets the historical nature of such disciplines. But why is that important? It is important because geometry expresses in its most pure form what Husserl calls 'the theoretical attitude', which is the stance that the natural sciences take towards their objects. Husserl's point is that to reactivate knowledge of the origin of geometry is to recall the way in which the theoretical attitude of the sciences belongs to a determinate social and historical context, what Husserl famously calls the 'life-world' (*Lebenswelt*). Husserl's critical and polemical point is that the activity of science has, since Galileo, resulted in what he calls a 'mathematization of nature', that overlooks the necessary dependence of science upon the everyday practices of the life-world. There is a gap between knowledge and wisdom, between science and everyday life. This is the situation that Husserl calls 'crisis', which occurs when the theoretical attitude of the sciences comes to define the way in which all entities are viewed. The task of philosophy, in Husserl's sense of the word (i.e. phenomenology), is to engage in a critical and historical reflection upon the origin of tradition that permits an active and reactivating experience of tradition against the pernicious naiveties of our present image of the past.

Matters are not so different in the early Heidegger's conception of *Destruktion,* the deconstruction of the history of ontology, which is precisely not a way of destroying the past, but rather of seeking the positive tendencies of the tradition and working against what Heidegger labels its 'baleful prejudices'. *Destruktion* is the production of a tradition as something made and fashioned through a process of repetition or retrieval, what Heidegger calls *Wiederholung.* The thought here is that a genuine relation to tradition is achieved through an act of retrieval or repetition, where one brings back the original meaning of a state of affairs through an act of critical and historical reflection. Heidegger's central example is the way in which the meaning of that which is – Being – is connected with time, a connection which he claims has been covered over in the tradition of

Western metaphysics since the time of the ancient Greeks. So, one has to destroy the received and banal sense of the past in order to experience the hidden and surprising power of history. In the period of *Being and Time* (the late 1920s), Heidegger articulates the difference between a received tradition and a destroyed one in terms of the distinction between tradition (*Tradition*) and heritage (*Überlieferung*). This does not mean, however, that tradition merges with some sort of heritage industry: rather Heidegger is playing on the senses of the German verb *überliefern* (to hand over, or deliver over), to suggest that an authentic relation to the past is one where its hidden potential is delivered over and disclosed. As such, for Heidegger, an authentic existence requires as its precondition a radical and not received experience of the past.

It is important to point out that the target of Husserl's and Heidegger's reflections on tradition – and this is equally true of Hegel's reflection on the history of Spirit and, as we will see presently, Nietzsche's conception of nihilism – is not the past as such, but the *present,* and precisely the *crisis* of the present. The true crisis of the European sciences or what Heidegger calls 'the distress of the West' is felt in the absence of distress: 'crisis, what crisis?' The real crisis is the absence of crisis, the real distress is the absence of distress. In such thoughtless amnesia, Dostoevsky might quip, we sink to the level of happy cattle. Thus, a reactivated or destroyed sense of the tradition – a radical tradition – permits us a critical consciousness of the present.

Philosophy as the production of crisis

One might say that the touchstone of philosophy in the Continental tradition is the question of praxis: that is to say, our historically and culturally embedded life as finite selves in a world that is of our own making. It is this touchstone of praxis that leads philosophy towards a critique of present conditions, as conditions not amenable to freedom, and towards the emancipatory demand that things be otherwise, the demand for a transformative practice of philosophy, art, thinking, or politics. Perhaps this fact begins to explain a possibly puzzling feature of philosophy in the Continental tradition, namely the theme of *crisis* that, in different forms, runs like an underground stream through the traditions of German idealism, Marxism, phenomenology, psychoanalysis, and the Frankfurt School. Such a mood of crisis can also be found in the culturally and politically more self-conscious areas of the analytic tradition. For example, it is evident in the Vienna Circle's fascinating 1929 Manifesto, which I shall discuss in Chapter 6. The authors argue for a scientific conception of the world and an overcoming of metaphysics as an essential element in a radical social democratic transformation of society.

For much of the Continental tradition, philosophy is a means to *criticize* the present, to promote a reflective awareness of the present as being in crisis, whether this is expressed as a crisis of faith in a bourgeois-philistine world (in Kierkegaard), a crisis of the European sciences (in Husserl), of the human sciences (in Foucault), of nihilism (in Nietzsche), of the forgetfulness of Being (in Heidegger), of bourgeois-capitalist society (in Marx), of the hegemony of instrumental rationality and the domination of nature (in Adorno and Max Horkheimer), or whatever. Philosophy as an acute reflection upon history, culture, and society leads to the awakening of critical consciousness, what Husserl would call the reactivation of a sedimented tradition. To push this a little further, the responsibility of the philosopher – in Husserl's formula 'the civil servant of humanity' – is the *production* of crisis, disturbing the slow accumulation of the deadening sediment of tradition in the name of a reactivating historical critique, whose horizon would be an emancipated life-world. Philosophy in the Continental tradition has an emancipatory intent. For a philosopher, the real crisis would be a situation where crisis was not recognized. In such a world, philosophy would have no purpose, other than as a historical curiosity, an intellectual distraction, or a technical means of sharpening one's common sense.

To try and formalize matters a little, let me propose the following simple model for philosophy in the Continental tradition, organized around the terms that make up the subtitle of this Chapter:

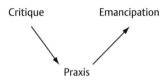

That is, critique is a critique of existing praxis because it is felt to be unjust, unfree, untrue, or whatever. Furthermore, it is a critique that aims towards an emancipation from that unjust praxis towards another individual or collective praxis, a different way of conceiving of human life, whether that is a Nietzschean life of solitary nobility, the communist society envisaged by Marx, the multiple becomings described by Deleuze and Guattari, or something completely different.

14. The tomb of Jean-Jacques Rousseau (1712–78) in the Pantheon, Paris

Chapter 5
What is to be Done?
How to respond to nihilism

As we saw in Chapter 2, Kant bequeathes a problem to his idealist, romantic, and even Marxist inheritors in the Continental tradition, a problem that he grapples with himself in the *Critique of Judgement* and which is at the core of Jacobi's critique of Kant and Fichte. The problem might now be put in the following way: the Kantian critique of metaphysics, if justified, achieves the remarkable feat of showing both the *cognitive* meaninglessness of the traditional claims of speculative, dogmatic metaphysics, while establishing the regulative *moral* necessity for the primacy of practical reason (that is, the concept of freedom). This raises the following question: how is freedom to be instantiated or to take effect in the world of nature, if the latter is governed by causality and mechanistically determined by the laws of nature? How is the causality of the natural world reconcilable with what Kant calls 'the causality of freedom'? How, to allude to Emerson alluding to the language of Kant's Third Critique, is genius to be transformed into practical power? Doesn't Kant leave human beings in what Hegel and the young Marx might have called the *amphibious* position of being both freely subject to the moral law and determined by an objective world of nature that has been stripped of any value and which stands over against human beings as a world of alienation? Isn't individual freedom reduced to an abstraction in the face of an indifferent world of objects that are available to one – at a price – as commodities?

15. Domenico Feti (1589–1624), 'Melancholy'

Such is the problem that Nietzsche diagnoses in the 1880s with the concept of nihilism – a concept that is absolutely decisive for a whole range of 20th-century Continental thinkers: Heidegger, Walter Benjamin, Theodor Adorno, Carl Schmitt, Hannah Arendt, Jacques Lacan, Michel Foucault, Jacques Derrida, and Julia Kristeva. Namely that the recognition of the subject's freedom goes hand in hand with the collapse of moral certainty in the world. In Chapter 2, we traced the emergence of this concept from Jacobi's critique of Kant and Fichte into Stirner, Dostoevsky, and Sartre. I would now like to go back to the theme of nihilism in more depth.

Russian nihilism

Nietzsche's understanding of nihilism has to be set in the Russian context alluded to in Chapter 2 with Dostoevsky – what he called 'nihilism à la Petersburg'. Nietzsche picked up the concept of nihilism from the Russian novelist Ivan Turgenev, read in Prosper Mérimée's French translation. Incidentally, Mérimée's 1845 novel *Carmen* also provided the basis for the libretto of Bizet's 1875 opera of the same name and Nietzsche's favourite – a highly disputable choice in my view, but that's another story. It is in Nietzsche's hands that nihilism receives its full philosophical statement and definitive expression.

What distinguishes the Russian context from the German one is that in the German version nihilism is largely a metaphysical or epistemological issue, whereas in the Russian it has a more obviously socio-political dimension. The story arguably begins with Nikolai Chernyshevski's attempt to 'nihilize' traditional aesthetic values by arguing that art is not the expression of some absolute conception of beauty, but rather represents the interests of a certain class at a certain point in history. Thus, in the Russian context, the problematic of nihilism is intimately linked to radical socialist politics, definitively expressed in Chernyshevski's hugely influential 1863 novel, *What is to be done?* The full story of the politics of Russian nihilism would have to include Michael Bakunin's anarchistic critique of the state, and perhaps culminate in Lenin's Promethean Bolshevism and the October Revolution of 1917. It is no coincidence that the 1902 book where Lenin describes his political vision of the party and the 'dictatorship of the proletariat' should also be entitled *What is to be done?*

In this sense, Russian nihilism is the expression of a radically sceptical, anti-aesthetic, utilitarian, and scientist world-view. Such a view is subjected to a genteel but devastating liberal critique in Turgenev's novel *Fathers and Sons* (1862) through the fate of the nihilist figure of Bazarov. The central dramatic conflict here is between two opposed world-views: the romanticism, liberalism, reformism, and Europhilia of the fathers (Nickolai and Pavel) and the positivism, utilitarianism, radicalism, and Russian nationalism of the sons (Arkady and Bazarov). Here we have the Russian expression of Mill's conflict between romanticism and utilitarianism, Bentham and Coleridge. In the central scene of the novel, amid vague intimations of nihilism as a force of violent insurrection, Bazarov sneers,

> 'We base our conduct on what we recognize as useful . . . In these days the most useful thing we can do is to repudiate – and so we repudiate.''Everything?'

> 'Everything.'

> 'What? Not only art, poetry . . . but also . . . I am afraid to say it . . .'

> 'Everything', Bazarov repeated with indescribable composure.

The dramatic conflict between liberalism and nihilism is classically, if unconvincingly, resolved by Turgenev: after falling powerfully, irrationally, and unrequitedly in love with Mme Odintsov – both an aristocrat and a romantic – Bazarov returns home to life as a country doctor like his father. In what amounts to an act of (logical, in Dostoevsky's sense) suicide, Bazarov contracts typhoid from the infected corpse of a peasant and confesses his love for Mme Odintsov on his deathbed. Thus, nihilism is overcome through the power of love and the novel ends with a Christian vision of 'everlasting reconciliation and of life which has no end'.

Nietzschean nihilism

The most succinct expression of Nietzsche's version of nihilism can be found in Book I of his posthumously assembled miscellany, *The Will to Power*. For Nietzsche, nihilism means,

> *That the highest values devalue themselves.* The aim is lacking; 'why' finds no answer.

What should be emphasized here is the use of the reflexive verb – 'devalue *themselves'*. Nietzsche is not claiming that the highest values are devalued through criticism, which would be Jacobi's or Turgenev's point. Rather it is intrinsic to their development that they have devalued *themselves*. This saying can be put alongside Nietzsche's most famous remark, scrawled on the former Berlin Wall and on toilet walls the world over, namely that 'God is dead'. This does not mean that God has somehow popped his clogs, quietly slipped out the back door of the universe without telling anyone, or that some other God has taken his place. Rather, it means 'we have killed him'. It is we humans who are culpable for the death of God. Nihilism is the breakdown of the order of meaning, where all that was posited as a transcendent source of value in pre-Kantian metaphysics becomes null and void, where there are no cognitive skyhooks upon which to hang a meaning for life. All transcendent claims for a meaning to life have been reduced to mere values – in Kant the reduction of God and the immortality of the soul to the status of postulates of pure practical reason – and those values have become incredible, standing in need of what Nietzsche calls 'transvaluation' or 'revaluation'.

Beyond any influence exerted from the Russian and German contexts, what must be emphasized is the sheer audacity and originality of Nietzsche's conception of nihilism. For Nietzsche, the cause of nihilism cannot be explained socially, politically, epistemologically, or even physiologically (i.e. in terms of some story about the decline of the species), but is rather rooted in a specific interpretation of the world: *Christianity*. For Nietzsche, the 'Christian-Moral' interpretation of the world had the distinct advantage of being an antidote to nihilism by granting the world meaning, granting human beings value, and preventing despair. However, for Nietzsche – and this is decisive – there is a paradox or antagonism within nihilism, namely that the Christian-Moral interpretation of the world is driven by a will to truthfulness, but that this very will to truth eventually turns against the Christian interpretation of the world by finding it untrue. That is to say, Christian metaphysics turns on the belief in a true world that is opposed to the false world of becoming that we inhabit here below. However, with the consciousness of the death of God, the true world is revealed to be a fable. Thus, and this is the paradox, the will for a moral interpretation or valuation of the world now appears to be a will to untruth. Christianity, like ancient tragedy in Nietzsche's early account in *The Birth of Tragedy*, does not so much die as commit suicide. And yet – here's the rub – a belief in a world of truth is *required* simply in order to live because we cannot endure this world of becoming. Nietzsche writes,

> But as soon as man finds out how that world is fabricated solely from psychological needs, and how he has absolutely no right to it, the last form of nihilism comes into being: it includes disbelief in any metaphysical world and forbids itself any belief in a *true* world. Having reached this standpoint, one grants the reality of becoming as the *only* reality, forbids oneself every kind of clandestine access to afterworlds

16. Friedrich Nietzsche (1844–1900) in military uniform

and false divinities – but *cannot endure this world though one does not want to deny it.*

This explains the central antagonism of nihilism for Nietzsche, namely that we are '*Not* to esteem what we know, and we are not *allowed* to esteem the lies we should like to tell ourselves'. That is, we can no longer believe in a world of truth beyond this world of becoming and yet we cannot endure this world of becoming. Or, to put this in terms that recall Jacobi's critique of Fichte, 'everything egoistic has come to disgust us (even though we realize the impossibility of the unegoistic); what is necessary has come to disgust us'. This vicious antagonism results in what Nietzsche calls 'a process of dissolution', namely that when we realize the shabby origin of our moral values and how the Christian-Moral interpretation of the world is driven by a will to untruth, our *reactive* response is to declare that existence is meaningless. It is this declaration of meaninglessness that Nietzsche identifies as nihilism and which he detects in three nascent forms:

1   In the pessimism of Schopenhauer, which Nietzsche calls 'passive nihilism' or, more injuriously, 'European Buddhism'. That is, if there is a void at the heart of my former metaphysical beliefs, then I might as well affirm the void and take up yoga, origami, or whatever.
2   In the Russian anarchism or 'active nihilism' that we saw in Turgenev and which Nietzsche sees as the mere 'expression of physiological decadence'. That is, if there is a void at the heart of my former metaphysical beliefs, then I can go on and destroy everything around me in acts of wildly creative terrorism. (This is a tendency within nihilism that one can detect in various extremist political movements like the Situationists in Paris in the 1960s, who claimed that because society is a mere spectacle, a hollow sham of empty seeming, the political task is one of announcing this fact in various, often highly aestheticized political acts. One of the famous Situationist slogans was, 'under the paving stones, it's a beach',

which entailed that one should uncover that beach by throwing those paving stones at the police.)

3   In a general cultural mood of weariness, apathy, exhaustion, and fatigue summarized in Nietzsche's memorable formula, 'Modern society . . . no longer has the strength to *excrete*'. That is, if there is a void at the heart of my metaphysical beliefs, then I might as well just shrug my shoulders and mutter, 'Oh well, I guess that's just the way it is'. We might think of this as 'armchair nihilism', classically expressed in the character of Eeyore in *Winnie the Pooh*.

But seriously, the essential point to grasp here is that nihilism is not simply the negation of the Christian-Moral interpretation of the world, but its *consequence*. For Nietzsche, nihilism as a psychological state is attained when we realize that the categories by means of which we had tried to give meaning to the universe are meaningless. This does not at all mean that the universe is meaningless, but rather, in a possible allusion to Kant, and a faint memory-trace of Jacobi, that 'the faith in the categories of reason is the cause of nihilism'. Thus, from a Nietzschean perspective, nihilism is the unforseen consequence of the Kantian critique of metaphysics. That is to say, nihilism is the consequence of moral valuation. My values no longer have a place in the world – it is this self-alienation of the modern Stoic that Hegel mockingly calls 'the moral view of the world'.

Now, such a position *can* lead to the resignation of passive nihilism or the enthusiastic delusions of active nihilism. But it can also lead to the demand for a revaluation of values, the transformative, emancipatory demand that things be different. In Nietzsche's work, and this is emblematic for a whole range of 20th-century Continental thinkers, the diagnosis of nihilism is accompanied by the demand for an overcoming of nihilism. Nietzsche's work is defined by its resistance to nihilism. This is why he repeatedly insists that new categories and new values are required that would permit us to endure this world of becoming without either falling into despair or inventing some new god and genuflecting before it.

As I see it, this is the function of the seemingly enigmatic doctrine of *eternal return* in Nietzsche's work, namely 'existence as it is, without meaning or aim, yet recurring inevitably without any finale of nothingness'. Nietzsche emphasizes that what is being attempted with the concept of eternal return is the very antithesis to pantheism. That is, if pantheism is the presence of God in all things, then eternal return is the attempt to think the universe consistently without God. Atheism for Nietzsche is not simply a statement of fact: it is also the consequence of considerable effort to free human beings from the idols to which they are wont to go cringing.

Although others would disagree, I see Nietzsche's concept of eternal return as a sort of hyper-Kantian thought experiment. That is, Kant's ethics is based on a notion of pure and sublime duty that cannot be based on any empirical interest, and cannot be viewed as the means to an end, such as happiness. Virtue has to be its own reward. And yet, Kant's ethics still retains God and immortality of the soul as postulates of pure practical reason. So, one's moral action can still in some sense be linked to the distant prospect of happiness where virtue would be rewarded. Nietzsche makes this initial Kantian thought more Kantian than Kant. For him, there is no God and the idea of the immortality of the soul is something of a bad joke. However, what Nietzsche asks of us with the thought of eternal return is to imagine our existence in a universe without theological meaning or metaphysical guarantee repeating itself endlessly, recurring eternally. Now, if we are the equal of *that* thought, that is, if we can know and still *affirm* such a picture, then we might well be able to say that we have finally overcome the nihilism that is implicit in the Christian-Moral interpretation of the world.

Dialectic of Enlightenment

To summarize: the historical and social condition of which nihilism is the diagnosis consists in the recognition of a double failure.

1   The values of modernity or Enlightenment do not connect with the fabric of moral and social relations, with the stuff of everyday life. That is, they fail to produce a new mythic or rational totality, what the authors of 'System-Programme' (see pp. 129–31) view as the need for a *mythology of reason*. In other words, Kant leaves us with a series of unreconciled dualisms. The moral values of Enlightenment (and this is the core of Hamann's and Hegel's critique of Kant which is inherited by the young Marx – where Enlightenment values becomes bourgeois values) lack any effectiveness, any connection to social praxis.

2   However, not only do the moral values of Enlightenment fail to connect with the fabric of moral and social relations, but – worse still – they lead instead to the progressive degradation of those relations through processes that we might call, with Max Weber, rationalization, with Marx, capitalization, with Adorno and Horkheimer, instrumental rationality, and with Heidegger, the forgetfulness of Being. Such is Enlightenment's fateful and paradoxical dialectic. As I see it, this is Jacobi's key insight and we have seen it unravelling through the story I have been telling.

Thus, to put it rather grandly, the problem of philosophical modernity, as presented so far, is how to confront the problem of nihilism after one has seen how the values of Enlightenment not only fail to get a grip on everyday life, but lead instead to its progressive dissolution. In my view, this is the problem that Continental philosophers return to again and again, either by trying to find a new way of responding to the problem, as for example in Habermas and Derrida, or by refusing the historical and philosophical terms in which the problem is posed, for example in Rorty.

Philosophy and non-philosophy

Of course, the further difficulty here is that such a confrontation with nihilism cannot simply take place in philosophy, if it is granted – as it is by thinkers as diverse as Nietzsche, Heidegger, and Adorno – that philosophy has conspired with the very forces that produce nihilism. For Nietzsche, philosophy is nihilistic; it is shot through with the asceticism and *ressentiment* of the Christian-Moral interpretation of the world. For Heidegger, as we will see below, traditional philosophy wants to know nothing of the nothing at the heart of its principle of suffcent reason. For Adorno, philosophy risks being an ideological discourse of abstraction that conspires with the abstraction of reified, commodified capitalist society.

How, then, does one respond to nihilism? That is the question. I have my own thoughts on the matter, as do other philosophers. All I have sought to establish thus far is that the response to nihilism is the substantive problematic of post-Kantian Continental philosophy, that runs like Ariadne's thread through the intellectual labyrinth of the last couple of centuries. It leads much Continental philosophy to look for non-philosophical discourses and practices that might respond to the crisis of modern times. Nietzsche finds resources in the tragic thinking of the Attic Greeks, Heidegger finds it in the meditative thoughtfulness of poetic creation, Adorno finds it in the autonomy of high modernist art, Marx finds it in political economy, Freud finds it on the couch in the practice of psychoanalysis. The point here is that the problematic of nihilism begins to explain why so much Continental philosophy is concerned with relations to non-philosophy, whether art, poetry, psychoanalysis, politics, or economics.

Progressive and reactionary modernism

After Nietzsche this concern with nihilism bifurcates into two different traditions of reflection on the crisis of the modern world, that can be coded as *progressive* and *reactionary* modernism. On the one hand, in the wake of Hegel's radical inheritors, like Ludwig Feuerbach and the young Marx, the philosophical critique of modernity merges with the more progressive German sociological critique of modernity that finds its definitive expression in the work of thinkers like Weber and Georg Simmel. This tradition continues with great fecundity in what is called 'Western Marxism' and the first generation of the Frankfurt School from the 1930s onwards. The most distinguished contemporary representative of this approach to modernity is Habermas, who held, significantly, a chair in philosophy *and* sociology at Frankfurt. This tradition continues to this day in the work of Habermas's successor at Frankfurt, Axel Honneth. Methodologically, this tradition is characterized by the belief in the reciprocal fertility of philosophy and sociology. That is, philosophical categories need to be sociologically mediated if they are to have any effectiveness; but sociological research requires the critical and reflective presence of philosophy to prevent it collapsing into positivism. Politically, this tradition of progressive modernism has been tied to various leftist currents of thought, whether Marxist or social democrat.

On the other hand, there is the more conservative critique of modernity that can be found in thinkers like Oswald Spengler, Carl Schmitt, and Ernst Jünger. In Spengler's formulation, the West is an 'ageing culture' that has entered an irreversible decline, like the late decadence of ancient Rome. The philosophical continuation of this tradition of social criticism in terms of a narrative of decline and collapse can be found in Heidegger, particularly in his reflections on technology from the late 1940s and 1950s. But also – unexpectedly perhaps – one can find this tradition of pessimistic cultural critique in Wittgenstein, who, in texts like *Culture and Value*, shows himself strongly influenced by Spengler. Whereas the methodology of progressive modernism is based on a mutual interdependence of philosophy and sociology, for the reactionary modernist sociology stands condemned as an expression of modern democratic decadence. Philosophical categories are, then, directly downloaded into social analysis which can produce a vertiginously pessimistic cultural diagnosis. Once again, Heidegger provides a classic example here, where he simply extends his thesis about the history of metaphysics as a forgetfulness of being into a cultural critique where all aspects of everyday life are dominated by a technological world picture that is the social expression of that same forgetfulness – 'the wasteland grows', as Heidegger sighs. The political consequences of reactionary modernism are well known in the case of Heidegger's commitment to National Socialism, in which he and others, like Schmitt and Jünger – however briefly – saw the practical possibility of an overthrow of nihilism. Needless to say, I do not find this a particularly savoury way of responding to the question posed in the title to this Chapter.

My point is that, despite their diametrically opposed political standpoints and significant methodological disagreements, both reactionary and progressive modernism are two responses to the problematic of nihilism. They are united in their belief that it is the business of philosophy to engage in what I have called the production of crisis. That is, philosophy is a critique of existing social praxis, as a variety of unfree or unjust praxis, that aspires towards some goal of individual or collective emancipation. The traditions differ – and differ utterly – in what they think such emancipation might consist in.

Chapter 6

A Case Study in Misunderstanding: Heidegger and Carnap

To utter a word and meaning nothing by it is unworthy of a philosopher.

Berkeley

My claim in Chapter 3 was that the best way of understanding the *mis*understanding between opposed philosophical traditions was in terms of the model of 'the two cultures'. According to this model, analytic and Continental philosophy can be seen as expressions of opposed, indeed antagonistic, habits of thought – Benthamite-empiricist-utilitarian and Coleridgean–hermeneutic–romantic – that make up the philosophical self-understanding of a specific culture. We saw, with Mill and Snow, how something like 'Englishness' might be understood in terms of this antagonism, and that, indeed, this might even prove to be a productive antagonism, provided that both sides to the conflict at least agree to talk with each other.

I now want to explore this line of thought a little further by considering a specific case study in the misunderstanding between traditions: the case of Heidegger and Carnap. Essentially, this is a dispute between the scientific conception of the world, advanced by Carnap and the Vienna Circle, and the existential or 'hermeneutic' experience of the world in Heidegger. This dispute is highly significant for subsequent developments in philosophy insofar as Carnap's views on Heidegger provide the background to Ayer's attempted logical positivist elimination of metaphysics in the British context, and Carnap had a vast influence on the professional development of analytic philosophy in the United States after the Second World War, not the least through his most celebrated student, W. V. O. Quine. For example, in an otherwise helpful little introduction to 20th-century philosophy, Ayer accuses Heidegger of 'what can fairly be described as charlatanism', based on a cursory reading of the 1929 lecture. And, in his eulogy after Carnap's death in 1970, Quine describes philosophy in the United States after the Second World War as 'post-Carnapian', rather than 'post-Wittgensteinian', which arguably described the comparable period in Britain. On the Continental side, Heidegger is undoubtedly a major inspiration behind the work of his German students, such as Hans-Georg Gadamer and Hannah Arendt, and on two generations of French thinkers like Sartre, Lacan, Foucault, and Derrida. As much of the recent misunderstandings between analytic and Continental philosophers can be traced back to this curious stand-off between Heidegger and Carnap, it is worth looking at in some detail.

Nothing comes of nothing

On 24 July 1929 Martin Heidegger gave his inaugural lecture as Professor of Philosophy at the University of Freiburg-in-Breisgau. He was 39 years old and at the height of his intellectual powers. He was returning to his home university after several enormously productive years in Marburg to take up the chair of his teacher, Edmund Husserl (with whom he would eventually break). It was a moment of clear personal triumph for Heidegger. The lecture had the deceptively simple title 'What is Metaphysics?', but was anything but simple. There is a story – doubtless apocryphal – that at the end of what must have been an arduous intellectual experience for those uninitiated in Heidegger's thought, there was a silence, broken by a question: 'Herr Heidegger, was ist Metaphysik?' ('Mr. Heidegger, what is metaphysics?'). To which Heidegger replied, 'Gute Frage!' ('Good question!').

17. Rudolf Carnap (1891–1970) and his wife Ina, Prague 1933

But what is metaphysics? Nietzsche famously defines metaphysics as
the division of one world into two. That is, the unity of the mythical
pre-philosophical experience of the world is sundered, with Plato, into
the realms of Being and seeming, reality and appearance, the
supersensible and the sensible. This is not wrong, but Heidegger
explicitly wants to return to a more Aristotelian understanding of
metaphysics. The word 'metaphysics' is not itself employed by Aristotle,
but is a term that has its origin in the classification of his works
undertaken in the library of Alexandria by Andronicus of Rhodes in the
2nd century. In the classification of the works of Aristotle, when his
works were arranged on the library shelf, as it were, there was the
Poetics, the Constitution of Athens, the political texts, the moral texts,

18. Martin Heidegger (1889–1976), looking surprised

the logical and rhetorical texts, etc. Then there were several books of physics, and after that there were a series of books signed by Aristotle which dealt with matters unclassifiable within the established schema. These books were called the 'after physics', in Greek *ta meta ta physika*.

But what comes after for Aristotle also came first, in the sense that what was dealt with in these books were the first principles that underwrote all other areas of enquiry. Aristotle's term for this fundamental area of philosophy was not metaphysics but *philosophia prote* (first philosophy). For Aristotle, there is a science or realm of knowledge (*episteme*) that deals with being as such. That is, it is not concerned with the being of any specific realm of things, such as living things (biology) or human society (politics), but with being as such in its universality and generality. The obsessive concern of Heidegger's thinking from beginning to end is the question of being, the question that is raised by metaphysical enquiry. Heidegger is concerned with being as such prior to its reference to any specific realm of beings or things. The maintenance of this gap between being as such and particular realms of beings is what Heidegger calls 'the ontological difference'.

Is Heidegger a metaphysician, then? Yes and no. He certainly appeared to be a metaphysician to Carnap and the Vienna Circle, and they were both right and wrong in this judgement. Heidegger is convinced that philosophical questions – and the question of being is, for him, *the* philosophical question – cannot be reduced to scientific enquiry. Therefore, metaphysics cannot be explained away by logical analysis: Heidegger can be seen to be retrieving the most fundamental question of ancient Greek philosophy, the question of being. However, Heidegger is *not* a metaphysician insofar as he believes that every philosophical system, from Plato to the present, in seeking to determine the meaning of being as such, has passed over the radicality of the *question* of being and the intrinsic link that this question has to the theme of time – hence the title of his magnum opus, *Being and Time*. For Heidegger, 'questioning is the piety of thinking'. The previous history of metaphysics has attempted to answer the being-question in various ways: for Plato, it is answered through the notion of 'form', namely that knowledge of a thing is knowledge of the form of a thing; for Aristotle, it is expressed with the notion of 'substance'; for Thomas Aquinas, it is answered with reference to the 'self-caused cause', that is God; for Hegel, it is 'Spirit'; for Nietzsche, it is 'will to power'; and so on. For Heidegger, the history of metaphysics is 'the history of being', a series of answers to the basic question of philosophy that extends from Plato to the inversion of Platonism in Nietzsche. Therefore, to raise the question of being radically is to place metaphysics in question and to pass over into its 'overcoming'. However, although Heidegger and Carnap both use the formula 'overcoming metaphysics', what they mean by it is strikingly different.

The basic orientation of the Vienna Circle can be expressed in the formula of Otto Neurath, a prominent member of the Circle: 'science free from metaphysics'. Philosophy is an under-labourer to science, solely concerned with the logical clarification of the propositions and method of empirical science. Indeed, one might go further and claim that the Vienna Circle does not practice philosophy at all, in the sense of advancing philosophical theses, but rather simply engages in logical analysis which clarifies the propositions of empirical science and criticizes the claims of traditional metaphysics. Neurath writes, 'there is no such thing as philosophy as a basic or universal science alongside or above the various fields of the one empirical science'. Reference to the 'one empirical science' alludes to the express goal of defining a scientific conception of the world, what Neurath called 'unified science'. This recalls Nietzsche's definition of metaphysics, where the scientific conception of the world would recover the unity of experience enjoyed in mythic world-views. Neurath speculates:

> The representatives of the scientific world-conception stand on the ground of simple human experience. They confidently approach the task

of removing the metaphysical and theological debris. Or, as some have it: returning, after a metaphysical interlude, to a unified picture of this world which had, in a sense, been at the basis of magical beliefs, free from theology, in the earliest times.

In relation to this scientific conception of the world, the propositions of metaphysics are not so much false as simply meaningless: they have no cognitive content. As such, they are the expression of legitimate feelings, but such feelings should have their proper medium in art, music, or poetry, rather than philosophy. Hence Carnap's cutting judgement that 'metaphysicians are musicians without musical ability'.

Now, in stark opposition to this conception of philosophy, Heidegger is going to offer a defence of metaphysics against science. Heidegger's question in the lecture is simple and powerful: 'What is happening to us, in the grounds of our existence, when science has become our passion?' His response is that when science becomes our passion, then there is a fragmentation and specialization of the various areas of knowledge, which leads to an atrophy of the metaphysical ground of scientific activity. Heidegger states categorically and not a little grandiloquently at the end of the lecture:

> Only if science exists on the basis of metaphysics can it fulfil in ever-renewed ways its essential task, which is not to amass and classify bits of knowledge, but to disclose in ever-renewed fashion the entire expanse of truth in nature and history.

Science has to be based in metaphysics – that much is clear. But what exactly is this basis? Well, it is *nothing*. But nothing comes of nothing, so what can this mean? This brings us to the controversial nub of Heidegger's ruminations, the question of the *nothing*, with which Carnap will have such malicious fun. Let me try and pick out the central thought from the baroque complexity of Heidegger's prose. In the first part of the lecture, Heidegger begins by claiming, uncontroversially enough, that the specific sciences deal with their particular realm of things, and besides that they are concerned with nothing. So, science wants to know everything about things or beings and besides that nothing. Heidegger then asks, perversely, 'what about this nothing?'. His claim is that science wants to know nothing about this nothing, whereas metaphysics, properly understood, might prove to be centrally concerned with this nothing. One can almost imagine Carnap sniggering like a schoolboy at the back of the lecture theatre, and his main critical point against Heidegger is that the question – 'what about this nothing?' – cannot even be formed in a logically consistent language for it turns a negation into some sort of spurious substantive. The fact that such a question can be formed at all is evidence that metaphysics feeds off certain ambiguities inherent in ordinary language that could and should be eliminated through logical reform. Such a logical reform of language was part of the early programme of the Vienna Circle.

Heidegger's next move is to look at how this question of the nothing is understood by traditional logic. The basic law of logic is the principle of non-contradiction, namely that it is contradictory to say that something can both be and not be at the same time. In accordance with this principle, logic conceives 'the nothing' as the negation of that which is or beings: not-x is the negation of x. As such, the metaphysical question of the nothing becomes a matter of negation. Without providing much in the way of argument, Heidegger states that 'the nothing is more originary that the "not" and negation'. Carnap will demur, but what Heidegger seems to mean here is that the logical understanding of 'the nothing' as negation conceives of negation theoretically with the intellect. Heidegger's point in the lecture (made in impressive detail in *Being and Time*) is that there are ways of conceiving things other than intellectually. He claims that prior to the theoretical disclosure of things, there is an affective or emotional disclosure that takes place in what Heidegger calls 'moods' – his translation of Aristotle's notion of *pathos*, (passion). Thus, a person is always in some sort of mood, whether depressed, elated, or simply indifferent, and the way he/she sees things is determined by this mood. For Heidegger, such moods cannot be understood as mere feelings, as some sort of psychological colouring in our otherwise rationally monochrome mental life. Moods define the way in which human beings experience their life in the world.

The question becomes, then: is there a mood that reveals the nothing? Heidegger's answer is yes and he claims that this is the function of *anxiety*, in German *Angst*. But surely one is always anxious about this or that: exams, a pathological fear of spiders, rats, or whatever. No, Heidegger insists, such specific anxiety is best called *fear*. When the cause – spiders, rats, exams – is removed, the fear disappears. Heidegger's point about anxiety is that it subsists and insists prior to all fear, like some uncanny background noise in one's existence. Anxiety is not, then, anxiety about this or that, it is anxiety about the whole of one's being. What happens in anxiety – and Heidegger's prose here takes on a wonderful descriptive force – is that all particular things slip away from one's grasp and one is left alone, feeling strange and uncanny. In the resulting experience of uncanniness, in the stillness and even calm that it produces, one feels the nothingness of all things and begins to ask the metaphysical question, first posed by Leibniz, 'why are there beings at all and why not rather nothing?'

So, for Heidegger, the nothing that opens in the experience of anxiety leads one to pose *the* metaphysical question as to the meaning of being. Odd as it sounds, the question of the nothing leads Heidegger straight into the heart of metaphysics, and such enquiry cannot be reduced to the scientific conception of the world propounded by the Vienna Circle. Philosophy is essentially metaphysics, and 'Philosophy can never be measured by the standard of the idea of science'. Heidegger concludes, 'Human Dasein (existence) can comport itself toward beings only if it holds itself out into the nothing. Going beyond occurs in the essence of Dasein. But this going beyond is metaphysics itself'. Science must be based on metaphysics.

The yellow brochure

1929 was a busy year in philosophy. On 15–17 September 1929, less than two months after Heidegger's lecture, there was a meeting of the Ernst Mach Association in Prague. It was decided to present a gift to Moritz Schlick (1882–1936), the *éminence grise* in what was to be baptized, with that gift, the Vienna Circle. Schlick had been away in Stanford as guest professor and had just turned down the offer of a chair in Bonn. The gift was a short text, essentially a manifesto, called 'The Scientific Conception of the World. The Vienna Circle'. The main text was anonymously authored, but the preface was signed by three members of the Circle: Hans Hahn, Otto Neurath, and Rudolf Carnap, although the radicalism of its content and the polemical tone of the prose reflect the views of Neurath, the most politically committed of the logical positivists. This little text would henceforth be known to initiates as 'the yellow brochure'.

What is most striking, given the conservatism of much of the analytic philosophy that would subsequently claim to be inspired by the Vienna Circle, is the stridently radical political character of the text. The scientific conception of the world is in conflict with reactionary metaphysical and theological tendencies in philosophy and politics. For the authors of the yellow brochure, the Vienna Circle 'faces modern times' by rejecting metaphysics and embracing empirical science. This development is intrinsically linked, in a manner reminiscent of Marx, with the emancipatory potential of the modern process of production. The Vienna Circle are at one with the masses insofar as 'their socialist attitudes tend to lead to a down-to-earth empiricist view'. The yellow brochure tells a short but persuasive story which traces the views of the Vienna Circle to various advances in the sciences, and engages in polemical attacks on counter-scientific, metaphysical tendencies. Its final words are, '*The scientific world-conception serves life, and life receives it*'. Such edifying statements make clear the danger that a thinker like Heidegger represents for the Vienna Circle. As Ayer telegraphically remarked in an enthusiastic letter sent from Vienna to Isaiah Berlin in 1933, 'All contemporary philosophers in Germany are rogues or fools. Even to think of Heidegger makes them sick'. For the Viennese positivists, Heidegger's work is the return to a reactionary, anti-scientific metaphysics, which is allied politically to pan-Germanic aspirations. The next decade would prove Carnap tragically justified in his suspicions, and all the prominent members of the Vienna Circle, many of whom were Jewish, left around the time of the *Anschluss* with Nazi Germany in 1936. As Bertrand Russell remarked, 'The severe logical training to which these men submitted themselves had, it appeared, rendered them immune to the infection of passionate dogma . . .'. In opposition to Heidegger's passionate political commitment to National Socialism in 1933, which was followed by a deepening quietism that has also troubled his followers, Carnap adopted consistently leftist views throughout his life, and indeed in the 1960s was active in the anti-racist movement in the USA. The politics of the Carnap–Heidegger conflict would seem to retain more than an echo of the Bentham–Coleridge debate analysed above.

Logic, empiricism, good poetry and bad

With this in mind, let's look in a little more detail at Carnap's 1932 essay 'Overcoming Metaphysics through Logical Analysis of Language', where he chooses Heidegger's 1929 lecture as a prime piece of metaphysical nonsense. Carnap's argument against metaphysics is not that its statements are false, but rather that they are simply meaningless. For logical positivists like Carnap, meaning is rooted in the principle of verification, namely that a word or sentence is meaningful only if it is in principle verifiable. But what are the conditions for verification? They are two-fold: logical and empirical.

For the Vienna Circle, following on from Russell and the early Wittgenstein, *logic* is a self-referential system that permits the reduction of all propositions to either tautologies or contradictions. To borrow the classical example: the proposition 'all bachelors are unmarried men' is a tautology for its predicate ('unmarried men') is interchangeable with or contained within its subject ('bachelors'). Such statements are what philosophers call 'analytic judgements'. Such judgements are true simply by virtue of their form, but they tell us absolutely nothing about what there is, about the facts. The opposite of a tautology is a contradiction, such as 'all bachelors are married men', which is by definition false; it also tells us nothing. So, all logical propositions are reducible to either tautologies or contradictions, which are either necessarily true or necessarily false, but all such propositions are verifiable and therefore meaningful. The only other realm of meaningful words or sentences is that of *empirical truth*. The early Wittgenstein believed that all empirical occurrences or complex states of affairs could be reduced to simple propositions that reflected the facts or the 'given'. If these simple or elementary propositions reflected the facts, then they could be verified against the facts. My proposition, 'this is a jacaranda tree' can be checked by simply looking at the beautiful huge green thing in front of me. Empirical propositions are verifiable and therefore meaningful.

Carnap's main claim in his 1932 paper is that metaphysical statements are neither logically nor empirically verifiable. For example, if I say that 'anxiety reveals the being of being human', then the logical positivist will ask, is this proposition logically verifiable? No, because it is neither a tautology nor a contradiction. So, is it then empirically verifiable? No, because 'being' is not a given fact like a jacaranda tree. Therefore the proposition is meaningless. And what goes for that proposition goes for all metaphysical propositions: if they are not verifiable, then they are meaningless and can be simply overcome through logical analysis.

But, it might be asked, if metaphysics is overcome, if, like Hume, we condemn all books containing unverifiable statements to the flames, then what role is left over for philosophy? Carnap insists that what is left is the method of logical analysis, and in a polemical essay from 1934 he states that 'the Vienna Circle does not practice philosophy'. But if Carnap is right (and that's a big 'if'), then how do we explain the fact that philosophers and non-philosophers have been preoccupied with metaphysical questions for thousands of years? Can so many people have been so stupid for so long? In the fascinating closing pages of his essay, Carnap, drawing on the views of Wilhelm Dilthey, answers this question by arguing that metaphysics is the expression of a feeling towards life, *Lebensgefühl*. In this respect, metaphysics is like art, which also gives expression to a feeling or attitude towards life. However – and here's the rub – metaphysics is inferior to art because the poet or musician does not imagine that their words or images have a theoretical or cognitive content. Therefore, metaphysics is bad art and metaphysicians are poets without poetic ability, musicians without musical ability. For Carnap, oddly enough, the thinker who best understood this problem was none other than Nietzsche, whose work either has some empirical content, such as his analyses of the history of morals, or does not choose to express itself in the form of theory, like Heidegger, but in the form of poetry. Carnap is obviously thinking of Nietzsche's *Thus Spake Zarathustra*, which attempts to respond to the philosophical problem of nihilism by adopting a non-metaphysical, mythical, even magical style.

The still hidden centre of philosophical conflict

Arne Naess wittily notes that, 'It would not be wholly unreasonable to say that Carnap reads Heidegger much as the devil would read the Bible'. This is no doubt true, but, as I have tried to indicate, Carnap and the Vienna Circle have understandable reasons for their Heidegger-bashing. The conflict between the scientific conception of the world and what Carnap sees as Heidegger's metaphysics is not just a theoretical disagreement, but also one expression of the social and political conflicts that so deeply scarred the last century. As far as I am aware, Carnap never returned to the conflict with Heidegger in his later work. But what did Heidegger say?

It is not, in my view, to be counted amongst Heidegger's virtues that he tended to treat his critics with haughty disdain, neglecting to engage with them head-on. Thus, there is only *one* parenthetical reference to Carnap in Heidegger's published work. However, there is a more indirect engagement with the sort of philosophical challenge that Carnap represents throughout his work. Heidegger tends to call this 'logistics' rather than logical analysis or analytic philosophy. In my view, one can imagine a debate with Carnap between the lines of Heidegger's texts that might raise the following four points:

1   Logical analysis is the most extreme expression of an objectified experience of language. That is, the living, breathing texture of everyday language is denuded into a formal, technical series of procedures. The attempted logical reform of language risks turning it into something unrecognizable by language users. In his work on language from the 1950s, Heidegger encourages us to undergo 'an experience with language' that cannot be captured in any formal metalanguage. Carnapian logical metalanguage would be as far from that experience as one could imagine.

2   The formalization of language in logical analysis transforms language into a technical instrument. The view of language adopted by Carnapian logical analysis is called 'metalinguistics' by Heidegger in the 1950s, and it is a view that he connects to his views on technology. Namely, Carnapian logical analysis belongs to that historical moment when philosophy becomes reduced to technical thinking. Heidegger adds, unforgettably, 'Metalanguage and sputnik, metalinguistics and rocketry are the same'. Logical analysis is at one with the will-to-power and domination of nature that defines the age of technology.

3   Carnap's attempt to overcome metaphysics by simply eliminating words like 'being' and 'nothingness' is, from a Heideggerian point of view, the expression of an unreflectively metaphysical view of the world. As mentioned above, Heidegger's view is that the history of metaphysics is the history of the forgetfulness of being.

The belief that the word 'being' should simply be struck from the register of meaning belongs, then, to the most extreme expression of this forgetfulness. Therefore, the Carnapian overcoming of metaphysics is just as metaphysical as the metaphysics it seeks to overcome.

4   In this sense, Carnap's praise for Nietzsche is rather revealing, for a Heideggerian might claim that logical analysis belongs to a sub-Nietzschean moment in the history of metaphysics. It might be recalled that Nietzsche writes, in *Twilight of the Idols*, 'But Heracleitus will always be right in this, that Being is an empty fiction'. Although Nietzsche would have seen logical positivism as a mere preliminary to his own overturning of Platonism.

At least, that is how one might *imagine* a Heideggerian responding to logical positivism. But let's go back to the one mention of Carnap in Heidegger's published work, because what he actually says is rather surprising. It appears in a 1964 letter published as a preface to a text written in the 1920s. Heidegger, exercising great restraint, speaks of,

> The still hidden centre of those endeavours towards which the 'philosophy' of our day, from its most extreme counter-positions [Carnap → Heidegger], tends. One calls these positions today: the technical-scientist view of language and the speculative-hermeneutic experience of language.

Now, I want to hear this quotation as Heidegger's expression of the two cultures problem in philosophy. That is, contemporary philosophy is agreed that language is the realm in which thinking takes place, but is at complete loggerheads as to how best to understand and describe that realm. For Carnap, it is a question of reforming the ambiguities and inconsistencies of everyday language in order to get a clear view of what can and cannot be said. For Heidegger it is a question of undergoing an experience with language that is sensitive to what takes place in everyday life.

Carnap's dogmas

It must not for a moment be imagined that the views of Carnap and the Vienna Circle enjoyed universal assent amongst analytic philosophers. Far from it. In a discussion on the relative merits of logical positivism with Brian Magee from 1982, Ayer wryly noted, 'Well, I suppose the most important defect was that nearly all of it was false'. In this respect, three problem areas can be briefly noted:

1   Carnap's criterion for distinguishing science from metaphysics is his verificationist theory of meaning. Karl Popper persuasively points out that such a notion of meaning is too narrow a criterion for making this distinction because many scientific theories are highly speculative. As evidence, he gives the example of Einstein: the theory of relativity is a speculative conjecture that simply cannot be reduced to a set of empirical observation statements. Indeed, the same might also be said about Newtonian dynamics, which was accepted as a theory not because it was empirically verifiable, but because it was the hypothesis with the greatest explanatory power. If Newton's or Einstein's views were later confirmed by observation, then so much the better. If not, they would have been refuted. A conjecture's veracity depends upon its capacity to withstand refutation. Thus, Popper's own criterion for the demarcation of science from metaphysics is refutability. If a theory is refutable, it is scientific; if it is irrefutable, it is metaphysical.

2   A second set of problems arises with the verification principle. First, in the face of critical attack, Carnap weakened his views from full empirical verification to a 'principle of confirmability'. In this view, sentences and words are meaningful if they are *in principle* confirmable by a *conceivable* observation. This is still an empirical criterion for meaning, although a little more relaxed than the earlier version. However, the real problem here is the status of the verification principle itself: if all propositions must be verified by

the verification principle, then how is this principle itself verified? That is, what is the verification of verification? Recall that, according to the verification principle, words and sentences are meaningful if and only if they are reducible to a tautology or are empirically observable. The verification principle cannot be an empirical statement because it is that by virtue of which such statements acquire meaning: the principle itself cannot be observed. Yet, it also cannot be a tautology, because although it is not itself a fact, it has a relation to the facts because it is the criterion according to which they are judged. A logical tautology can by definition have no relation to the facts. Thus, if it is neither tautological nor factual, then how may one verify the verification principle? The only option is that it would have to be somehow self-verifying, which means that it would have to be able to make statements about itself and provide its own argument. This all begins to sound rather like the old-fashioned metaphysics that Carnap and the Vienna Circle wished to overcome. The problem here can be put more colourfully: the verification principle is a modern version of Occam's Razor, which shaves off superfluous metaphysical entities from the realm of empirical facts. The question is: how can this razor shave itself? If a razor cannot shave itself, then we cannot *a fortiori* verify verification. The verification principle is a performative self-contradiction.

3   But the most formidable objections to Carnap were advanced by his student Quine in his celebrated paper 'Two Dogmas of Empiricism' (1951). The first dogma of empiricism consists in the feasibility of the distinction between logical tautologies and empirical observation statements – what is known technically as the analytic–synthetic distinction. The second dogma is what Quine calls 'radical reductionism', namely that every empirical statement is reducible to a statement about the facts or the given. Quine's claim is that the second dogma cannot be sustained, and if this is so, then the first dogma also falls. Hence, Carnap's entire picture of meaning collapses. In Wilfrid Sellars's language, Carnap

and the Vienna Circle are seduced by 'the myth of the given', by the idea that words and sentences have a direct relation to an immediately available reality. Quine presents an alternative picture of the relation of beliefs to experience, likening the whole of our knowledge to 'a man-made fabric which impinges on experience only along the edges'. The consequence of this view is a much more holistic picture of the relation of beliefs to experience, or concepts to intuitions, that Quine describes as a 'thorough pragmatism'. Although Quine went on in his later work to qualify his early views in much more strongly naturalistic terms, it is with this pragmatist critique of empiricism that Richard Rorty has made fascinating connections to the Continental philosophical tradition.

Wittgenstein thinks he knows what Heidegger means

As we have seen, much of the heat of this encounter turns on the question of metaphysics, with Carnap denouncing Heidegger as a metaphysician and Heidegger implying that Carnap's scientific conception of the world presupposes an unexamined metaphysics. Thus, they both accuse the other of the same metaphysical fault. Such evident bad manners are nothing new in the history of philosophy. But as a way of mediating these opposed positions, let me turn to a little fragment by Wittgenstein, also from 1929, where, in response to Heidegger's lecture, he says,

> To be sure, I can readily think what Heidegger means by being and anxiety. Man feels the urge to run up against the limits of language. Think for example of the astonishment that anything at all exists. This astonishment cannot be expressed in the form of a question, and there is no answer whatsoever. Anything we might say is *a priori* bound to be mere nonsense. Nevertheless we do run up against the limits of language.

It is perhaps helpful here to think of Wittgenstein as a mediating third party in the conflict between Heidegger and Carnap. Although the Vienna Circle's programme of logical analysis was largely inspired by Wittgenstein's *Tractatus*, relations between Wittgenstein and the Vienna Circle were never easy and Wittgenstein suddenly and inexplicably broke off contact with Carnap in 1929. Also, after Wittgenstein's return to philosophy in the late 1920s, his views underwent a rapid change that increasingly distanced him from the Vienna Circle. Pre-empting Quine, Wittgenstein came to regard the views of the *Tractatus* as dogmatic. Thus, if the early Wittgenstein was held captive by a picture of language reducible to logic that enabled one to say what could be said while passing over the remainder in silence, then the later Wittgenstein sought to escape this picture by analysing ordinary language usage. As he puts it in the *Philosophical Investigations*, 'Don't look for the meaning, look for the use'. That is, the central philosophical concern becomes the understanding of language in its pragmatic everydayness. We don't need to invent a new language because the one we have is perfectly sufficient.

Wittgenstein used to recount an anecdote from his conversations with G. E. Moore in Cambridge, where their dialogue concentrated on the following problem: must we comprehend logical analysis in order to understand what we mean by the propositions of ordinary language? Wittgenstein responded to Moore with the words, 'What an infernal idea!' In this sense, with Heidegger in mind, we might see the later Wittgenstein as seeking to move away from formal metalanguage and towards an experience of language as such. So, if Carnap's attempted overcoming of metaphysics is based on the views of the early Wittgenstein, then the later Wittgenstein represents what might be called 'an overcoming of overcoming', where we would put aside the dogmas of logical analysis and return to ordinary language and the human social life expressed in that language in all its messy but rich everydayness.

However, one should not imagine that Wittgenstein was some sort of happy Heideggerian. Nothing could be further from the truth. It is clear that his comment entails a significant critique of Heidegger. That is, Wittgenstein thinks he knows what Heidegger means by being and anxiety, but implies that such things cannot be said without falling into nonsense. In a Wittgensteinian view, what Heidegger is trying to do in the 1929 lecture is to say the unsayable by running up against the limits of language. Now, for Wittgenstein, nonsense is a serious business and testifies to deep desires in human beings, which he would describe as ethical. But what Heidegger is saying is nonsense nonetheless, which was Carnap's point after all. 'What is Metaphysics?' is a classic example of language on holiday. So, the fact that Wittgenstein knows what Heidegger means by being and anxiety does not necessarily mean that these terms mean what Heidegger thinks they mean.

To my mind, the interest of the Heidegger–Carnap conflict does not consist in deciding who is right and who is wrong, but rather in viewing

19. Jacques Callot (1592–1635), 'Les deux "pantalons"'

that conflict as a definitive expression of both a philosophical problematic and a cultural pathology that are still very much with us. If this is not recognized, then we risk a fruitless philosophical stalemate, namely the stand-off between scientism on the one hand and obscurantism on the other. The topic of the next chapter is to try and find a way through this stand-off and approach the still hidden centre of philosophy of which Heidegger speaks.

Chapter 7

Scientism versus Obscurantism: Avoiding the traditional predicament in philosophy

True philosophy consists in relearning to look at the world.

Maurice Merleau-Ponty

As I argued in Chapter 4, the fact that so much philosophy in the Continental tradition can be said to respond to a sense of crisis in the modern world, and to attempt to produce a critical consciousness of the present with an emancipatory intent, goes some way to explaining its most salient and dramatic difference from much analytic philosophy, namely its *anti-scientism*. From a Continental perspective, the adoption of scientism in philosophy fails to grasp the critical and emancipatory function of philosophy: that is, it fails to see the possible complicity between a scientific conception of the world and what Nietzsche saw as nihilism. It fails fundamentally to see the role that science and technology play in the alienation of human beings from the world. This alienation can happen in a number of ways, whether through turning the world into a causally determined realm of objects that stand against an isolated human subject, or through turning those objects into empty commodities that can be surveyed or traded with indifference.

The critique of scientism resides in the belief that the model of the natural sciences cannot and, moreover, should not provide a model for philosophical method, and that the natural sciences do not provide human beings with their primary and most significant access to the world. One finds this belief expressed in a whole range of Continental thinkers, such as Bergson, Husserl, Heidegger, and the philosophers associated with the Frankfurt School from the 1930s onwards. In this connection, Habermas's book *Knowledge and Human Interests* (1968) cannot be recommended too highly. For Habermas, scientism means science's belief in itself: that is, 'the conviction that we can no longer understand science as *one* form of knowledge, but rather must identify knowledge with science'. *Knowledge and Human Interests* is a systematic critique of scientism that proceeds historically by reconstructing the emergence of positivism out of the reception of Kant's critical philosophy in the mid-19th century, in the work of Ernst Mach and Auguste Comte. Essentially, Habermas recounts the prehistory of the Vienna Circle's scientific conception of the world, but his intent is both critical and emancipatory. He argues that positivism and scientism constitute the disavowal of any notion of critical reflection, the kind of reflection embodied in the work of Kant and in the German idealist development of that critical project that provided the basis for an emancipatory social theory in Marx, Weber, and the early Frankfurt School. What Habermas means by this claim is that Kant's critical philosophy is (as we saw in Chapter 2) a reflection on the conditions of possibility of a knowing, speaking, and acting subject. Kant is thus seeking to establish the foundations for theoretical, scientific knowledge, but his transcendental enquiry has an emancipatory point insofar as it seeks to defend the concept of human freedom. As Habermas remarks, 'the act of self-reflection that "changes a life" is a movement of emancipation'. Hegel then takes this critical project a stage further by reflecting upon the ways in which Kant's philosophy has to presuppose a whole set of contextually embedded assumptions rooted in the actually existing lifeworld and the structures and history of social life. That is, the Kantian picture of *knowledge* has to presuppose a whole series of *interests* that are not adequately reflected upon – this is the basis for Hegel's claim that Kantian ethics, despite its laudable intention, remains a context-free, abstract formalism. It is Habermas's contention that, after Hegel, this notion of critical reflection on the relation of knowledge to interest is picked up in an exemplary way by Freudian psychoanalysis, despite Freud's unfortunate tendency towards scientism, which Habermas does his best to excise. That is, psychoanalysis is a critical, reflective practice which seeks to emancipate human beings from the various illusions with which they are wont to delude themselves, and 'by understanding these illusions the subject emancipates itself from itself'.

Doing phenomenology

There is, however, a danger that a legitimate worry about scientism can develop into an anti-scientific attitude. This is the risk of *obscurantism*. In my view, the two poles that are to be avoided in philosophy are scientism and obscurantism, which reflect pernicious tendencies within both analytic and Continental philosophy, as the conflict between Carnap and Heidegger so eloquently shows. In Heidegger's only allusion to Carnap, he spoke of 'the still hidden centre' of thinking between the opposed counterpositions of contemporary philosophy. I now want to try and think about that centre by defending a notion of phenomenology that aims to undermine scientism without falling into obscurantism.

Merleau-Ponty, in a nice turn of phrase, describes the task of phenomenology as 'unveiling the pre-theoretical layer' of human experience upon which the theoretical attitude of the scientific conception of the world is based. It is something like Merleau-Ponty's conception of phenomenology that I would like to defend here. In my understanding, it is a question of *doing* phenomenology in order to try and uncover the pre-theoretical layer of the experience of persons and things and to find a mode of felicitous description for this layer of experience with its own rigour and standards of validity. It is this obdurate yet almost intangible dimension of pre-theoretical experience

20. Otto Mühl, 'Oh Sensibility' (1925)

that phenomenology has the job of elucidating, the mystery of the familiar that Merleau-Ponty tried to articulate with the notion of 'the perceptual faith'. That is, when I open my eyes and look around at the world, I have complete faith that it both exists and is richly meaningful. The problem is that this faith breaks down when I start to reflect on it and ask myself, 'Well, how can I be certain that there is an external world for me when the evidence of my senses is not always completely reliable?' How does one regain the naivety of the perceptual faith when one has already attained the standpoint of reflection? Merleau-Ponty answers this problem with a notion of what he calls 'hyper-reflection': that is, phenomenology is reflection upon what precedes reflection, the pre-theoretical substrate of experience. The point here is that access to the pre-theoretical level of human experience is not necessarily immediate for human beings like us who have attained the theoretical attitude of the sciences. Phenomenology therefore implies relearning to see the world in all its palpable and practical presence.

Pre-science

So, how can phenomenology avoid both scientism and obscurantism? Let me begin with scientism. In my view, *scientism* rests on the fallacious claim that the theoretical or natural scientific way of viewing things provides the primary and most significant access to ourselves and our world, and that the methodology of the natural sciences provides the best form of explanation for all phenomena. Phenomenology shows that the scientific conception of the world, in Carnap and Neurath, say, is parasitic upon a prior practical view of the world as pre-reflectively there in a handy, matter-of-fact sort of way. This world is what we might call the *environment* (in German *Umwelt*), the world that surrounds us, which is closest, most familiar, and most meaningful to us. This environing world is not the value-neutral objective world of science, but the world that is always already coloured by our cognitive, ethical, and aesthetic values. That is to say, scientism, or what Husserl calls objectivism, overlooks the phenomenon of the *life-world* as the enabling condition for scientific practice. In *The Crisis of the European Sciences*, Husserl describes the life-world in the following way,

> It belongs to what is taken for granted, prior to all scientific thought and all philosophical questioning, that the world is – always is in advance – and that every correction of an opinion, whether an experiential or other opinion, presupposes the already existing world, namely as a horizon of what in the given case is indubitably valid as existing ... Objective science, too, asks questions only on the ground of the world's existing in advance through prescientific life.

The critique of scientism within phenomenology does not seek to refute or negate the results of scientific research in the name of some mystical apprehension of the unity of man and nature, or whatever. Rather, it simply insists that science does not provide the primary or most significant access to a sense of ourselves and the world. Anti-scientism does not at all entail an anti-scientific attitude, nor does it mean that 'science does not think', a late remark of Heidegger's that has caused more problems than it has solved. In my view, what is required here is what the young Heidegger called, in a much-overlooked but highly suggestive remark from *Being and Time*, 'an *existential conception of science*'. This would show how the practices of the natural sciences arise out of life-world practices, and that the life-world practices are not simply reducible to natural scientific explanation.

Let me develop this point a little further with reference to Heidegger's notion of what he calls 'pre-science' (in German *Vor-wissenschaft*). In a stunningly clear lecture from 1924, which contains in embryonic form many of the arguments of *Being and Time*, Heidegger describes his reflections as belonging to a pre-science that would be an interpretative elucidation of the conditions of possibility for scientific research. What Heidegger means by this is that a pre-science describes the social genesis of the theoretical attitude of the sciences in the practices of the life-world. In what I shall generously assume is an attempt at humour on

Heidegger's part, he describes this pre-science as the police force at the procession of the sciences, conducting an occasional house search of the ancients and checking whether scientific research is indeed close to the things themselves, and hence phenomenological, or whether science is working with a traditional or handed-down knowledge of its matters. One imagines the mass arrest and detention of whole crowds of naturalistically minded philosophers by such a phenomenological police force. Elsewhere in Heidegger, this phenomenological policing is called a *productive logic*. That is, it is a pre-scientific disclosure of the life-world that lays the ground for the sciences by leaping ahead of them. What Heidegger would seem to mean here is that, unlike the empiricist or Lockean conception of the philosopher as an under-labourer to science (as discussed in Chapter 1), a productive logic leaps ahead of the sciences by showing their basis in a phenomenology of persons, things, and world, the pre-theoretical layer of experience.

What I have called 'a phenomenological pre-science' or 'an existential conception of science' does not dispute or refute the work of the sciences. It shows that the theoretical attitude of the sciences finds its condition of possibility in our various life-world practices – in Habermas's terms, theoretical knowledge is rooted in practical interests. Furthermore, as will become clearer below, it shows that such practices require interpretative clarification or a hermeneutics, and not the causal hypotheses of natural science or the causal-sounding explanations of pseudo-science. What phenomenology provides is a clarifying redescription of persons, things, and the world we inhabit. As such, phenomenology does not produce any great discoveries, but rather gives us a series of reminders of matters with which we were acquainted, but which become covered up when we assume the theoretical attitude of the natural sciences. Phenomenology provides what we might call 'everyday anamnesis', a recollection of the background practices and routines that make up the delicate web of ordinary life.

The *X-Files* complex

Let me turn now to obscurantism. It is important to point out that such a phenomenological anti-scientism *can* lead to an anti-scientific *obscurantism*, which in many ways is the inverted or perverted counter-concept to scientism, but it *need* not do so if we are careful enough to engage in a little intellectual policing. Obscurantism might here be defined as the rejection of the causal explanations offered by natural science by referring them to an alternative causal story, that is somehow of a higher order, but essentially occult. That is, obscurantism is the replacement of a scientific form of explanation, which is believed to be scientistic, with a counter-scientific, mysterious, but still causal explanation – the earthquake was not caused by plate tectonics but by God's anger at our sinfulness.

As a cultural phenomenon, this is something that can be observed in every episode of *The X-Files*, where two causal hypotheses are offered, one scientific, the other occult, and where the former is always proved wrong and the latter right, but in some way that still leaves us perplexed. That is, the paranormal phenomenon in question can be explained, but its cause is still enigmatic – it's a mystery. Now, as a cultural distraction, arguably this does little harm, but elsewhere the effects of the *X-Files* complex can be more damaging. Familiar candidates for obscurantist explanation are the will of God, the ubiquity of alien intelligence, the action of the stars on human behaviour, and so on. Less obvious, but arguably equally pernicious candidates are the drives in Freud, Jung's archetypes, the real in Lacan, power in Foucault, *différance* in Derrida, the trace of God in Levinas, or – indeed – the epochal withdrawal of being in and as history in the later Heidegger. This list might be extended.

In my view, what we can still learn from phenomenology is that when it comes to our primary and most significant access to persons and things – what we might call our entire stock of tacit, background know-how about the social world – we do not require causal scientific explanations, or pseudo-scientific hypotheses in relation to obscure causes, but what I am tempted to call, thinking of Wittgenstein, *clarificatory remarks*. For example, 'The aspects of things that are most important for us are hidden because of their simplicity and familiarity. (One is unable to notice something – because it is always before one's eyes)'. Clarificatory remarks bring into view features of our everyday life that were hidden but self-evident, and hidden because they were self-evident. They make these phenomena more perspicuous, change the aspect under which they are seen, and give to matters a new and surprising overview. In this sense, phenomenology is a reordering of what was tacitly known but went unnoticed; it permits us to relearn how to look at the world. Of course, viewing Heidegger's work in this way does not sound as exciting as talking about the epochal donation of being in its withdrawal or whatever, but perhaps that sort of excitement is something we are best off without.

It should be clear from what I have been saying that I am attempting a mini-pathology of the contemporary philosophical scene, which is meant to comment on – and maybe curb – the worst excesses of both Continental and analytic philosophy. On the one hand, there is a risk of obscurantism in some Continental philosophy, where social phenomena are explicated with reference to forces, entities, and categories so vast and vague as to explain everything and nothing at all. For example, a phenomenon like the internet (or mobile phones or even mobile homes) might be seen as further evidence in support of Heidegger's thesis on what he calls the *Gestell*, the enframing attitude that prevails in the technological world and thereby tributary to the forgetfulness of being. As such, everyday phenomena are seemingly explained with reference to causal-sounding agencies which function something like the gods in ancient mythology. Any aspect of personal and public life might be seen as evidence of the disciplinary matrices of power, the disintegration of the 'Big Other' and the trauma of the real, the multiple becomings of the body without organs, or whatever. Where such obscurantist tendencies exist, then the therapy has to be demystification or demythologization. That is, there must be a critique of this kind of talk and an investigation into why we engage in it in the first place.

But, on the other side of my mini-pathology, there is the risk of a chronic scientism in some areas of analytic philosophy. If we can imagine a philosophical paper with the title 'Qualia and Materialism: Closing the Explanatory Gap', then why not papers with titles like, 'The Big Bang and Me: Closing the Explanatory Gap' or 'Natural Selection and Me: Closing the Explanatory Gap'? The assumption of such scientistic approaches is that there is a gap that can be closed through a better empirical explanation. It has been my contention throughout this book that there is a felt gap here – the gap between knowledge and wisdom – that cannot be closed through empirical enquiry. That is, the question of the meaning of life is not reducible to empirical enquiry. This felt gap between knowledge and wisdom is the very space of critical reflection. In philosophy, but also more generally in cultural life, we need to clip the wings of both scientism and obscurantism and thereby avoid what is worst in both Continental and analytic philosophy. That is, we need to avoid the error of believing that we can resolve through causal or causal-sounding explanation what demands phenomenological clarification. Of course, this is much easier said than done, but at least we could make a start.

Of course, the distinction between scientism and obscurantism is not as neat as I might have suggested. First, obscurantism might not be a single thing. There is indeed the obscurantism based on faith in some sort of numinous enigma, whether Zeus, Yahweh, or the death drive – what might be called 'obscure obscurantism'. But there are other obscurantisms which style themselves scientifically provable: 'Doctor, can't you see that my sleeplessness and aggression is caused by the fact that I was abducted by aliens when I was camping last summer?'; or 'Just one more year of research and I will finally have proved that matter is the product of divine effusions'. And of course there are scientisms which are taken on faith and are thus the equivalent of obscurantism. For example, I might believe that all mental states can be reduced to evolutionary dispositions without knowing how or why. It just feels right. We might call this an 'obscure scientism', or whatever. Let's just say that there is a pressing need for a more detailed taxonomy of the scientism/obscurantism distinction.

A little intellectual policing

If we are going to be capable of approaching the still hidden centre between the two philosophical cultures described in this book, then I think we need to engage in a little intellectual policing. That is, we need to return to the classical distinction, first coined by Max Weber, between explanation and clarification, between causal or causal-sounding hypotheses and demands for elucidation, interpretation, or whatever. In brief, Weber's claim is that natural phenomena require causal explanation, while social phenomena require clarification by giving reasons or offering possible motives as to why something is the way it is. One of the jobs of philosophy is to remind us that we urgently need to make this distinction, and that if we don't then we will end up in the stale stand-off we saw between Heidegger and Carnap, and risk falling into either scientism, obscurantism, or the tempting twilight zone of the *X-Files* complex. It has been my contention in this chapter that the best way of ensuring we make this distinction is through an unthrilling but compelling version of phenomenology, but there are doubtless other ways of achieving this end. My point has been nicely put by Hilary Putnam, a philosopher from the analytic tradition who has been increasingly vocal in his criticism of scientism in philosophy,

> I think that Aristotle was profoundly right in holding that ethics is concerned with how we live and with human happiness, and also profoundly right in holding that this sort of knowledge ('practical knowledge') is different from theoretical knowledge. A view of

knowledge that acknowledges that the sphere of knowledge is wider than the sphere of 'science' seems to me to be a cultural necessity if we are to arrive at a sane and human view of ourselves and of science.

We live with – and within – a gap between knowledge and wisdom. It is time philosophers, and everyone else, started to try and think about that gap. Maybe more than our personal peace of mind is at stake.

Chapter 8

Sapere aude:

The exhaustion of theory and the promise of philosophy

It is agreeable to imagine a future in which the tiresome 'analytic-Continental split' is looked back upon as an unfortunate temporary breakdown of communication – a future in which Sellars and Habermas, Davidson and Gadamer, Putnam and Derrida, Rawls and Foucault are seen as fellow-travellers on the same journey . . .

Richard Rorty

I think that it is at least arguable that the present state of philosophy is interestingly marked by the exhaustion of a whole series of theoretical paradigms. Analytical philosophy, as I mentioned above, has happily achieved some historical self-consciousness and become interested in its own tradition, as well as realizing that there is indeed a compelling story to be told about Germanophone philosophy between Kant and Frege. But one wonders whether this is too little too late, and whether the interest in the origins, the history, or indeed the Hegelian prehistory of analytic philosophy, as well as the current vogue for post-analytic philosophy, are simply attempts to shut the stable door after the horse has bolted.

In the German context, the Frankfurt School after Habermas's retirement is rather uncertain about its present agenda and future direction, and it is often difficult to see what now distinguishes it from broader mainstream movements in Anglo-American moral and political philosophy and social theory. Of course, this was the implicit point of much post-war German philosophy: normalization after the catastrophe of National Socialism. More widely, Germany is philosophically somehow becalmed, and the great post-war generation of Habermas, Karl-Otto Apel, Ernst Tugendhat, Michael Theunissen, Dieter Henrich, and Niklas Luhmann are almost all either deceased or retired, and their successors have not yet reached their intellectual heights.

And let's face it, Paris is not what it was. The collapse of neo-Kantianism in France in the 1930s and the rise of what the French called '*les trois H*' (Hegel, Husserl, Heidegger) produced two generations of stunning intellectual brilliance. In the first generation, one thinks of Levinas, Sartre, de Beauvoir, Merleau-Ponty, Lévi-Strauss, Lacan, Bataille, and Blanchot. In the second generation, one thinks of Althusser, Foucault, Derrida, Deleuze, Lyotard, and Kristéva. But while Derrida is still very much going strong, and there is plenty of interesting philosophical work going on (in particular the renaissance of French moral and political philosophy) and an intriguing renewal of phenomenology, one has the impression that none of this is exactly going to set the world alight.

Of course, this poses problems for the usual idea of Continental philosophy. The once-justified professional insider rationale was that there was a philosophical tradition extending from German idealism and romanticism, through to phenomenology, hermeneutics, and the Frankfurt School, which was either forgotten, suppressed, or simply ignored by the dominant analytic approach. In this sense, and with a gesture that is utterly English, and which can be traced back to Mill and Arnold, it is a question of importing foreign prince(sse)s from over the water, of illuminating the dour utilitarianism of the island with a little Continental sweetness and light. But Continental philosophy itself, as I understand it and have tried to explain it, faces two substantial problems: first, as already indicated, there is not *that* much interesting work going on across the Channel; and second, much of the tradition that was ignored is now being interestingly read and used by analytically trained philosophers who are working on the ground prepared by philosophers like Taylor, Cavell, and Rorty.

To one ruminating in a millennial mood, it is unclear quite what the future holds philosophically, if anything at all. But to look on the bright side, I would like to conclude the book with a couple of possible remedies for the present situation. Let's go back to where my story started, with Kant. Kant summarized the project of Enlightenment in the words *sapere aude*, which might be freely rendered: *dare to think for yourself*. That is, Continental philosophers cannot, and in my view, should not, expect any new prince(sse)s from over the water. We cannot expect to import the next grand Continental paradigm from Frankfurt, Paris, or wherever.

We have to think for ourselves philosophically, which is, of course, an extremely hazardous business. But I think such work is beginning and I would even say that there is emerging, in Britain and elsewhere in the English-speaking world, a genuine and non-sectarian recurrence of interest in deep philosophical issues informed by both major traditions, and a sense that these issues must be addressed to local conditions and learn to speak the dialect of the place and the language of the tribe. Part of the problem is that Continental philosophy has been reduced to a list of proper names, with various competing methodologies attached, that one could survey with enthusiasm, bewilderment, or indifference during one or a series of introductory courses, or by reading books like this one. In my view, it is no longer a question of worshipping a series of proper names, but of *doing something* with what they left behind; doing creative, inventive thematic work and not restricting oneself to translation and commentary. Philosophy must be clearly argued conceptual creation in critical relation to given traditions of thinking, and not a melancholic mourning for missed opportunities or a mere technique for sharpening one's common sense.

As I have tried to show, the current divisions in the study of philosophy are a consequence of certain more or less inadequate professional self-descriptions. Both Continental and analytic philosophy are, to a great extent, sectarian self-descriptions that are the consequence of the professionalization of the discipline, a process that has led to the weakening of philosophy's critical function and its emancipatory intent, and to its progressive marginalization in the life of culture. As such, to borrow Rorty's word, the distinction has become tiresome.

The story I have tried to tell in this book is how this distinction can be related back to a more interesting historical picture where analytic and Continental philosophy can be viewed as vital expressions of the problem of 'the two cultures': scientific explanation versus humanistic interpretation, empirical–scientific–Benthamite–Carnapian versus hermeneutic–romantic–Coleridgean–Heideggerian. My claim has been that when this cultural situation is not properly understood, then we risk getting stuck in a rather fruitless, and indeed pernicious, stand-off between scientism on the one hand, and obscurantism on the other. To understand aright the two-cultures problem in philosophy we have to understand the divergent paths that philosophy took after Kant and the different problems that came to define it. I have tried to sketch the Continental side of the story by focusing on the theme of the crisis of reason after Kant and describing the problematic of nihilism that this provokes. My hope is that once this story has become clear and we have learned to overcome any lingering sectarianism, then we might begin to move on philosophically and face up to issues of deep and enduring intellectual interest, such as those concerned with the gap between knowledge and wisdom.

Finally, this is what I want to offer as the promise of philosophy, as a promise that can hopefully be kept: that philosophy might form an essential part in the life of a culture, in how a culture converses with itself and with other cultures. Philosophy is that moment of critical reflection in a specific context, where human beings are invited to analyse the world in which they find themselves, and to question what passes for common sense in the particular society in which they live by raising questions of the most general form: 'What is justice?', 'What is love?', 'What is the meaning of life?'. Even more crudely stated, the hope is that the various considerations to which such questions give rise can, through enquiry and argumentation, have an educative, emancipatory effect. As Stanley Cavell notes, philosophy is the education of grown-ups. But this should hardly be news, as it is a description of philosophy that would not have surprised Socrates.

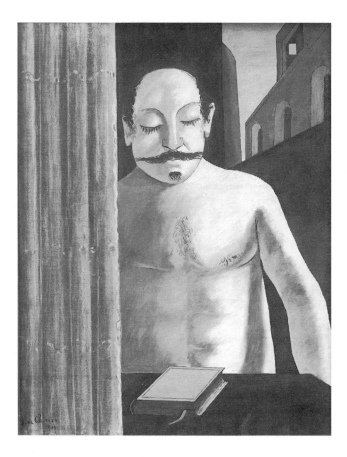

21. Giorgio de Chirico (1888–1979), 'The Child's Brain'

Appendix

The so-called 'Oldest System Programme of German Idealism' (1796)

recto

An Ethics. As the whole of metaphysics will in future come under *Morality* – of which Kant only gave an *example* with his two practical postulates and *exhausted* nothing, this ethics will be nothing but a complete system of all Ideas, or, which is the same, of all practical postulates. The first Idea is naturally the notion *of my self* as an absolutely free being. With the free self-conscious being [*Wesen*] a whole *world* emerges at the same time – out of nothing – the only true and thinkable *creation from nothing* – Here I will descend to the fields of physics; the question is this: how must a world be for a moral being? I should like to give wings again to our physics which is progressing slowly and laboriously via experiments.

Thus – if philosophy gives the Ideas and experience the data we can finally achieve the grand physics which I expect from later epochs. It does not appear that our present physics could satisfy a creative spirit which is like ours, or like ours should be.

From nature I come to *human activity* [*Menschenwerk*]. Putting the Idea of humanity first – I want to show that there is no Idea of the *State* because the state is something *mechanical*, just as little as there is an Idea of a *machine*.

Only that which is an object of *freedom* is called an *Idea*. We must, then, also go beyond the state! – For every state must treat free people as a piece of machinery; and it should not do this; this it must *come to an end*.

You can see yourselves that here all the Ideas, of eternal peace etc. are only *subordinate* Ideas of a higher Idea. At the same time I want here to establish the principles for a *History of Mankind* and to completely expose the whole miserable human creation of state, constitution, government, legislature. Finally come the Ideas of a moral world, divinity, immortality – the upturning of all superstition, the pursuit of the priesthood, which has recently been feigning reason, by reason itself. – Absolute freedom of all spirits who bear the intelligible [*intellektuelle*] world in themselves, and may not seek either God or immortality *outside themselves.*

Finally the Idea which unites all, the Idea of *beauty*, the word taken in the higher platonic sense. I am now convinced that the highest act of reason, which embraces all Ideas, is an aesthetic act, and that *truth and goodness* are brothers *only in beauty* – The philosopher must possess just as much aesthetic power

verso

as the poet [*Dichter*]. People without aesthetic sense are our pedantic philosophers [*BuchstabenPhilosophen*]. The philosophy of spirit is an aesthetic philosophy. Once cannot be spiritual [*geistreich*] in anything, one cannot even reason spiritually about history – without aesthetic sense. It should here become apparent what it is that people lack who understand no Ideas – and admit faithfully enough that everything is a mystery to them as soon as it goes beyond charts and registers.

Poetry thereby gains a higher dignity, at the end it again becomes what it was at the beginning – *teacher of (History) mankind*; for there is no philosophy, no history any more, poetry alone will survive all the remaining sciences and arts.

At the same time we hear so often that the masses should have a *sensuous religion*. Not only the masses but also the philosopher needs monotheism of reason of the heart, polytheism of imagination [*Einbildungskraft*] and of art, this is what we need!

First of all I shall speak here of an Idea which, as far as I know, has never occurred to anyone – we must have a new mythology, but this mythology must be in the service of the Ideas, it must become a mythology of *reason*.

Before we make the Ideas aesthetic i.e. mythological, they are of no interest to the *people* and on the other hand before mythology is reasonable the philosopher must be ashamed of it. Thus enlightened and unenlightened must finally shake hands, mythology must become philosophical and the people reasonable, and philosophy must become mythological in order to make the philosophers sensuous. Then eternal unity will reign among us. Never the despising gaze, never the blind trembling of the people before its wise men and priests. Only then can we expect the *same* development of *all* powers, of the individual as well as all individuals. No power will be suppressed any more, then general freedom and equality of spirits will reign! – A higher spirit sent from heaven must found this new religion among us, it will be the last, greatest work of mankind.

From Andrew Bowie, *Aesthetics and Subjectivity: From Kant to Nietzsche* (Manchester University Press, Manchester, 1990). Translation by Andrew Bowie.

References

Chapter 2

Michael Dummett, *Origins of Analytical Philosophy* (Duckworth, London, 1993)

Frederick Beiser, 'The Context and Problematic for Post-Kantian Philosophy', in *A Companion to Continental Philosophy* (Blackwell, Oxford, 1998)

F. H. Jacobi, 'Open Letter to Fichte', trans. D. I. Behler, in *Philosophy of German Idealism*, ed. E. Behler (Continuum, New York, 1987)

Max Stirner, *The Ego and Its Own*, ed. D. Leopold (Cambridge University Press, Cambridge, 1995)

Jean-Paul Sartre, *Being and Nothingness*, trans. Hazel Barnes (Routledge, London, 1958)

Fyodor Dostoevsky, *The Devils*, trans. D. Magurshak (Penguin, Harmondsworth, 1971)

Dostoevsky, *The Diary of a Writer*, trans. B. Brasol (George Braziller, New York, 1954)

Chapter 3

David E. Cooper, 'Modern European Philosophy', in *The Blackwell Companion to Philosophy* (Blackwell, Oxford, 1996)

Bernard Williams, 'Contemporary Philosophy: A Second Look', in *The Blackwell Companion to Philosophy* (Blackwell, Oxford, 1996)

Stanley Rosen, *The Question of Being. A Reversal of Heidegger* (Yale University Press, New Haven, 1993)

A. J. Ayer, *Part of my Life* (Collins, London, 1977)

Georges Bataille, 'Un-knowing and its consequences', in *October*, no. 36 (1986)

The Oxford Companion to Philosophy, ed. Ted Honderich (Oxford University Press, Oxford, 1995)

John Searle, 'Contemporary Philosophy in the United States', in *The Blackwell Companion to Philosophy*, ed. Nicholas Bunnin and E. P. Tsui James (Blackwell, Oxford, 1996)

Mill and Bentham, *Utilitarianism and Other Essays*, ed. Alan Ryan (Penguin, Harmondsworth, 1987)

Mill, *Autobiography*, ed. J. Stillinger (Houghton Mifflin, Boston, 1969)

C. P. Snow, *The Two Cultures* (Cambridge University Press, Cambridge, 1998)

Stephen Toulmin, *Cosmopolis* (University of Chicago Press, Chicago, Ill., 1990)

Note: I owe the discussion of Ayer and Bataille to conversations with Juha Himanka, and I owe the reference to Mill's essay on Coleridge to Jonathan Rée.

Chapter 4

Richard Rorty, *Contingency, Irony, and Solidarity* (Cambridge University Press, Cambridge, 1989)

Stanley Cavell, *The Claim of Reason* (Oxford University Press, Oxford, 1979)

Richard Rorty's Introduction to Sellars' *Empiricism and the Philosophy of Mind* (Harvard University Press, Cambridge, Mass., 1997)

The Analytic Tradition, eds. David Bell and Neil Cooper (Blackwell, Oxford, 1990)

Ray Monk, *Ludwig Wittgenstein. The Duty of Genius* (Jonathan Cape, London, 1990) and *Bertrand Russell: The Spirit of Solitude* (Jonathan Cape, London, 1996)

Michael Ignatieff, *Isaiah Berlin* (Chatto and Windus, London, 1998)

Ben Rogers, *A. J. Ayer. A Life* (Chatto and Windus, London, 1999)

Rudiger Safranski, *Martin Heidegger. Between Good and Evil* (Harvard University Press, Cambridge, Mass., 1998)

Georg Lukács, *Soul and Form* (Merlin, London, 1974)

Jacques Derrida, *Edmund Husserl's 'Origin of Geometry': An Introduction*, trans. J. P. Leavey (University of Nebraska Press, Lincoln, Nebr., 1989)

Martin Heidegger, *Being and Time,* trans. J. Macquarrie and E. Robinson, (Blackwell, Oxford, 1962)

'Wissenschaftliche Weltauffassung: Der Wiener Kreis' in Otto Neurath, *Empiricism and Sociology* (Reidel, Dordrecht, 1973)

Chapter 5

Kant, *The Critique of Judgement*, trans. James Creed Meredith (Oxford University Press, Oxford, 1952)

Emerson, 'Experience', in *Selected Essays,* ed. L. Ziff (Penguin, Harmondsworth, 1982)

Turgenev, *Fathers and Sons*, trans. R. Edmonds (Penguin, Harmondsworth, 1965)

Nietzsche, *The Will to Power*, trans. Walter Kaufmann and R. J. Hollingdale (Vintage, New York, 1968)

Hegel, *Phenomenology of Spirit*, trans. A. V. Miller (Oxford University Press, Oxford, 1977)

Chapter 6

Martin Heidegger, *Pathmarks*, ed. William McNeill (Cambridge University Press, Cambridge, 1998)

Rudolf Carnap, 'The Elimination of Metaphysics Through Logical Analysis of Language', in *Logical Positivism*, ed. A. J. Ayer (Free Press, Glencoe, Scotland, 1959)

Carnap, *The Unity of Science* (Thoemmes Press, Bristol, 1995)

Arne Naess, *Four Modern Philosophers. Carnap, Wittgenstein, Heidegger, Sartre* (University of Chicago Press, Chicago, 1968)

Heidegger, *On the Way to Language* (Harper and Row, New York, 1971)

Karl Popper, 'The Demarcation Between Science and Metaphysics', in *The Philosophy of Rudolf Carnap* (Open Court, La Salle, 1963)

W. V. O. Quine, *From a Logical Point of View* (Harvard University Press, Cambridge, Mass., 1980)

Wilfrid Sellars, *Empiricism and the Philosophy of Mind* (Harvard University Press, Cambridge, Mass., 1997)

Wittgenstein, 'On Heidegger on Being and Dread', in *Heidegger and Modern Philosophy*, ed. Michael Murray (Yale University Press, Newhaven, Conn., 1978)

Chapter 7

Jürgen Habermas, *Knowledge and Human Interests*, trans. Jeremy J. Shapiro (Polity Press, Cambridge, 1987)

Maurice Merleau-Ponty, 'The Philosopher and his Shadow', in *Signs* (Northwestern University Press, Evanston, Ill., 1964)

Edmund Husserl, *The Crisis of the European Sciences* (Northwestern University Press, Evanston, Ill., 1954)

Martin Heidegger, *Being and Time* (Blackwell, Oxford, 1962)

Heidegger, *The Concept of Time*, transl. W. McNeill (Blackwell, Oxford, 1992)

Wittgenstein, *Philosophical Investigations*, transl. G. E. M. Anscombe (Blackwell, Oxford, 1958)

Frank Cioffi, *Wittgenstein on Freud and Frazer* (Cambridge University Press, Cambridge, 1998)

Hilary Putnam, *Meaning and the Moral Sciences* (Routledge, London, 1978)

Further Reading

For compendious recent surveys of the entire Continental philosophical tradition beginning with Kant and German idealism, see Simon Critchley and William Schroeder (eds), *A Companion to Continental Philosophy* (Blackwell, Oxford, 1998) and Simon Glendinning (ed.), *The Edinburgh Encyclopedia of Continental Philosophy* (Edinburgh University Press, Edinburgh, 1999). I have expanded material from the Introduction to the Blackwell's Companion in drafting this book. Chapter 7 of this book appeared in a different form in the *Times Higher Education Supplement*, 6 February 1998, under the title 'Dare to Think'. For helpful single-volume summaries of the Continental tradition, see Robert Solomon, *Continental Philosophy Since 1750* (Oxford University Press, Oxford, 1988) and David West, *An Introduction to Continental Philosophy* (Polity Press, Cambridge, 1996). For anthologies containing extracts from primary texts, see Richard Kearney and Mara Rainwater (eds), *The Continental Philosophy Reader* (Routledge, London, 1996) and Karen Feldman and William McNeill (eds), *Continental Philosophy: An Anthology* (Blackwell, Oxford, 1997).

The argument of Chapter 1 was suggested to me by three books: Pierre Hadot, *Philosophy as a Way of Life* (Blackwell, Oxford, 1995), Stephen Toulmin, *Cosmopolis* (University of Chicago Press, Chicago, Ill., 1990), and John Cottingham, *Philosophy and the Good Life* (Cambridge University Press, Cambridge, 1998). Also, on the question of the relation of science to the meaning of life, Dostoevsky's *Notes from Underground* was frequently on my mind, a text which is a better introduction to philosophy than most.

The argument of Chapter 2 was strongly influenced by Michael Dummett's *Origins of Analytical Philosophy* (Duckworth, London, 1993) and Frederick Beiser's *The Fate of Reason: German Philosophy from Kant to Fichte* (Harvard University Press, Cambridge, Mass., 1987). For an overview of the shape and progress of German idealism and romanticism, see the six essays in 'The Kantian Legacy' in the Blackwell *Companion to Continental Philosophy*. See also Steven Crowell's essay on 'Neo-Kantianism' in the same volume. For a very useful overview of German romanticism and idealism and their relevance for contemporary philosophy, see the work of Andrew Bowie, especially *Aesthetics and Subjectivity* (Manchester University Press, Manchester, 1990). John Stuart Mill's essays on Bentham and Coleridge, discussed in Chapter 3, can be found in *Utilitarianism and Other Essays* (Penguin, Harmondsworth, 1987). On the question of two cultures, see Stefan Collini's very helpful introduction to *The Two Cultures* (Cambridge University Press, Cambridge, 1998).

Chapter 4 begins by mentioning Rorty and Cavell. The best introduction to their work is their own writings; see Rorty's now classic book, *Philosophy and the Mirror of Nature* (Princeton University Press, Princeton, NJ, 1980) and Cavell's wonderfully rich *The Claim of Reason* (Oxford University Press, Oxford, 1979). On the question of tradition and on much else, see Husserl's classic *The Crisis of European Sciences and Transcendental Phenomenology* (Northwestern University Press, Evanston, 1970) and the 'Introduction' to Heidegger's *Being and Time* (Blackwell, Oxford, 1962).

Turning to Chapter 5, for a helpful discussion of nihilism before Nietzsche, see Michael Gillespie's *Nihilism Before Nietzsche* (University of Chicago Press, Chicago, Ill., 1995). On nihilism in Nietzsche, see Mark

Warren, *Nietzsche and Political Thought* (MIT Press, Cambridge, Mass., 1988) and Keith Ansell-Pearson, *Nietzsche as a Political Thinker* (Cambridge University Press, Cambridge, 1994). For my own thoughts on how to respond to nihilism, see *Very Little . . . Almost Nothing* (Routledge, London, 1997).

For the Heidegger–Carnap controversy discussed in Chapter 6, Carnap's essay can be found under the title 'The Elimination of Metaphysics through Logical Analysis of Language', in *Logical Positivism*, ed. A. J. Ayer (Free Press, Glencoe, 1959). The most accurate translation of Heidegger's 'What is Metaphysics?' can be found in *Pathmarks*, ed. William McNeill (Cambridge University Press, Cambridge, 1998). The interesting 'Postscript' and 'Introduction' to 'What is Metaphysics?' can also be found in the same volume. The 'Yellow Brochure' can be found in Otto Neurath, 'The Scientific Conception of the World' (1929) in *Empiricism and Sociology* (Reidel, Dordrecht, 1973).

The argument of Chapter 7 on the problem of scientism and obscurantism was inspired by the work of Frank Cioffi: see his *Wittgenstein on Freud and Frazer* (Cambridge University Press, Cambridge, 1998). See also Habermas, *Knowledge and Human Interests* (Polity Press, Cambridge, 1987) and Richard Bernstein, *Beyond Objectivism and Relativism* (University of Pennsylvania Press, Philadelphia, Pa., 1983). For the classic statement of the relation between causal explanation and interpretative understanding, see Peter Winch, *The Idea of a Social Science and its Relation to Philosophy* (Routledge, London, 1990).

On the notion of philosophy as conceptual creation alluded to in Chapter 8, see the opening chapters of Deleuze and Guattari's wonderful *What is Philosophy?* (Columbia University Press, New York, 1994).

Index

Expand your collection of
VERY SHORT INTRODUCTIONS

Available now

1. Classics
2. Music
3. Buddhism
4. Literary Theory
5. Hinduism
6. Psychology
7. Islam
8. Politics
9. Theology
10. Archaeology
11. Judaism
12. Sociology
13. The Koran
14. The Bible
15. Social and
    Cultural Anthropology
16. History
17. Roman Britain
18. The Anglo-Saxon Age
19. Medieval Britain
20. The Tudors
21. Stuart Britain
22. Eighteenth-Century Britain
23. Nineteenth-Century Britain
24. Twentieth-Century Britain
25. Heidegger
26. Ancient Philosophy
27. Socrates
28. Marx
29. Logic
30. Descartes
31. Machiavelli
32. Aristotle
33. Hume
34. Nietzsche
35. Darwin
36. The European Union
37. Gandhi
38. Augustine
39. Intelligence
40. Jung
41. Buddha
42. Paul
43. Continental Philosophy
44. Galileo
45. Freud
46. Wittgenstein
47. Indian Philosophy

Available soon

Ancient Egypt
Animal Rights
Art Theory
The Brain
Chaos
Cosmology
Design
Drugs
Economics
Emotion
Ethics
Evolution
Evolutionary Psychology
Fascism
The Fall of the Soviet Union
The First World War
Free Will
International Relations
Mathematics
Modern Ireland
Molecules
Northern Ireland
Opera
Philosophy
Philosophy of Religion
The Russian Revolution
Terrorism
World Music

Visit the
VERY SHORT
INTRODUCTIONS
Web site

www.oup.co.uk/vsi

➤ **Information** about all published titles

➤ News of **forthcoming books**

➤ **Extracts** from the books, including titles not yet published

➤ **Reviews** and views

➤ **Links** to other **web sites** and main OUP web page

➤ Information about **VSIs in translation**

➤ **Contact** the editors

➤ **Order** other **VSIs** on-line